Philip James Bailey

The International Policy of the Great Powers

Philip James Bailey

The International Policy of the Great Powers

ISBN/EAN: 9783337816056

Printed in Europe, USA, Canada, Australia, Japan

Cover: Foto ©Suzi / pixelio.de

More available books at **www.hansebooks.com**

THE

INTERNATIONAL POLICY

OF THE

GREAT POWERS.

BY PHILIP JAMES BAILEY,

AUTHOR OF ' FESTUS.'

LONDON:

SAUNDERS, OTLEY, AND CO.,

66, BROOK STREET, HANOVER SQUARE.

1861

LONDON: PRINTED BY W. CLOWES AND SONS, STAMFORD STREET,
AND CHARING CROSS.

CONTENTS.

	PAGE
AUSTRIA	3
PRUSSIA	41
GERMANY AND SCANDINAVIA	65
RUSSIA	101
FRANCE	157
GREAT BRITAIN	211

PREFACE.

THE principal Powers of Europe are identical with three great races,—the Kelt, the Teuton, and the Sclave ; and these in their primary aspects and main branches and combinations constitute the general sum of Continental population. All came from the East, as is supposed, and in the order above indicated. The East, indeed, appears to have thrown off its masses of humanity as the sun is thought by some philosophers to have projected from its surface the planetary bodies of the universe; and, like these, the former also became wanderers. Whatever there may be among the celestial, among the earthly wayfarers the ruling principle was apparently, at the outset, less attraction than repulsion; and such to a great degree — notwithstanding separate and defined positions—it still continues.

The outward tendency of civilization has always manifestly been westward; and while those peoples more strictly called Eastern, because there more permanently situated, have rapidly arrived at a certain degree of eminence, and then become stationary or retrograde, the nations of the West, though dating their civilization later in life, have always shown—at least during the historic period—a more elastic and progressive career.

Of these, even, some are far more advanced than others in the arts, the elegancies of life, and the general results of civilization, both substantial and refined. But in this very superiority—it is obvious to the lightest reflection —is partly involved a danger of a most serious nature—it might almost be characterised as a fatality, the history of the world upon this point being painfully explicit. It seems, therefore, almost incumbent upon those nations who have consciously attained to a certain pitch of civilization, either to prepare for a gradual but sensible decline, from the consequences of over-refinement, over-stimulated intellect, or minutely-divided industry; or, springing back to that position from which the race originally started, to cultivate, in some degree at least, those warlike aspirations and propensities which are the universal instinct of humanity in its present condition, and which, however apparently incompatible with reason, were probably implanted there for some good purpose.

In vain morality abjures, philanthropy abhors, religion condemns, war. The traditions of man's heart are unfortunately all in favour of it; and nations not unfrequently draw the sword as their most solemn manifesto. War indeed is sometimes felt to be a necessity, irrespective of success; sometimes

a glory, independent of its object. No doubt
this is a sad reflection, but it forces itself
upon the mind. There are times when moral
influence is sufficient for the adjustment of
affairs between nations, or within their own
separate confines; and well it is when a people
can obey contentedly the solemn mandates of
a Solon, or a Samuel; or even listen assentingly
to the admonitions of a Burke, wisest of merely
human legislators ; but periods constantly
recur in the history of the world when the
only accepted authority is that of the sword.

The profession—if anything could. it might
be thought—of a common religion would have
tended, if not sufficed, in compliance with the
imitative and emulative propensities of the
human mind. not only to a greater resemblance
in internal institutions, but to a more marked
approximation towards the moral standard of
that Divine code by which the several nations
affirm themselves to be bound ; but it has not

so proved ; for, while at different æras, on doctrinal points—many of which were altogether
beyond the range of the understanding—the
various sections of Christendom have indulged
in the bitterest animosities and the fiercest and
most deadly persecutions, they have recently,
abandoning all controversy, moral or mystical,
agreed simply to ignore altogether the plainest
and least debateable precepts of their religion ;
so that, by implied assent of all, not only may
nominal professors practise, but the priests of
every Church may preach, and the purists of
every denomination justify, those enormities
which are the natural efflorescence of the
warlike passions ; and they thereby virtually
proclaim either their own inconsistency or
the utter powerlessness of their faith to control
the proclivities of our original constitution.
Christianity, in fact, is confessed by all the
peoples in Europe ; and so sincerely, that it
is never appealed to when its decision might

be effective. Mankind has, therefore, yet to see, and to consent to, the introduction of an influence capable practically of diverting the grand current of the world's affairs from those channels in which they have hitherto uninterruptedly flowed from the days of Nimrod to Napoleon,—the channels of ambition, and interest, and luxury, and national aggrandisement.

If a philosophic mind, speculative rather than sceptical, should here pause for a moment to inquire why this should be so; why the supposed interests of different nations should so far diverge as, in the face of Christianity and philanthropy, to lead to a policy of unremitting reciprocal hostility, the answer may unhappily too readily be found in the conclusion furnished by experience: that the ineradicable diversities of race, original varieties of temperament, of social habits, nay, even of mental processes, sow in themselves the seeds of permanent antagonism; that sentiments, sympathies, and antipathies are as ultimate and irresolvable facts as the genera of animals and minerals in the mixed constitution of the world; that charity or philanthropy, the only common bond which religion supplies for our dealings with others of the same or different creed, is, when applied to masses of men, wholly inoperative; that the highest development of the species appears in somewise inextricably involved in the attempt to achieve by force a national, or tribal predominance; that however false to their faith, men must be true to their nature; and that just reason, no doubt identical with true religion, whose holy and united influence should subdue or chastise the fatal discord of the inferior elements of our nature, never is, like the *prima materies* of philosophy, to be found in its pure or original shape; but asserted only by the theorist and believed in solely by the neophyte, is never

humanly beheld except as disguised by sophists
or distorted by fanatics; corrupted by the ignorance of peoples, or rendered contemptible by
the presumption of kings.

When, if ever, in the lapse of generations,
mankind shall, not the less, emerge from
the night of national antipathies and the
dubious twilight of cherished animosities into
the broad day of universal sympathy, and
the pure and hallowed light of a charitable
and practical religion; when strife shall have
refined itself into competition, and competition become elevated into emulation; when
the mysterious stream of time, so often tur-
bid with the blood of nations, shall have
been changed by the priest and prophet of a
regenerated humanity into a river rolling with
gold,—the gold of peace, and wisdom, and
felicity: history will doubtless be enabled to
trace, under the inspiration of her Divine Interpreter, in one continuous and luminous

narrative, the gradual conversion or the sudden transmutation of these elements and bases of society, whereby every separate agency of civilization shall be shown to be identical with the finger of Providence, and the hand of man the veritable stamp and impress of the hand of God. But, while the world awaits that change, to us, and to any save of enthusiastic and momentary vision, much of this is impracticable. The key to the past is still hidden in the future; we can only accept the relations of things as they are.

AUSTRIA.

B

AUSTRIA.

AUSTRIA, the successor of the Holy Roman Empire, for a long period the centre of European policy and always of diplomatic activity, forms, with its component nationalities, races, and religions, a vast and complex Power, outwardly at least compact; the exigencies of whose condition it is impossible to contemplate without deep interest; and the permanence of whose position as a leading Power is apparently and simply a beneficial necessity.

With one third of her population Evangelical Protestants, Greek Catholics, and Jews, the solid majority, still attached to the Church of Rome, have always given to Austria a preponderating influence in matters of religion throughout Central Europe; as her long and severe contests, both internally and externally, with Bohemians, Swedes, and others, and her want of sympathy at the time with her only hitherto reforming Emperor, sufficiently testify. Notable for obedience to ecclesiastical authority, Austria, by her recent Concordat with Rome, assumed a somewhat reactionary attitude; but its operation, having been perceived to be inimical to the common equality and impartial toleration of different forms of religion which had been for a long time effectually established throughout the empire, has been in all directions judiciously restricted. The position of the Church in its spiritual capacity and authority, as well as in certain matters relating to temporalities, not being satisfactory, it was only natural and just that the ruling powers at Rome and Vienna should seek a reconciliation of their interests; and that while the former was redoubling its exertions, through the many legitimate channels at its disposal, for the conservation of the secular power in its present form and circumstances, the Emperor, wishing to displace, by priestly help, the tendencies of the people to press upon the springs of government, had, in reality, by surrendering certain privileges to the Church, aimed, by diminishing his power, to increase his influence. But although in Austria, as everywhere else, a reaction has taken place during the last twenty years in favour of the Church, and although it thus became necessary to reinaugurate a freer and more perfect connection between the national Church and its spiritual head, yet, considering the temper of the times with regard to religious dogmas and sacerdotal authority, the Imperial government acted unwisely in permitting suddenly so great a change, and at the same time magnifying it by authoritative announcement. Measures such as this, and treated in such manner, are beyond all doubt profoundly impolitic. Like damp gunpowder, they may be totally inoperative; they may be fearfully explosive. In such circumstances the Church enlarges her dignity by not exerting her authority; which could only have the effect of adding to social antagonism and political passion that bitterest and most subtle of human sentiments which in different circumstances the laity of all communions distinguish by names indicative of various degrees of execration, but the bigots of all sects agree to denominate zeal.

The main characteristic of Austrian policy, both in its domestic and foreign aspects, is well known; it is the support of what is called legitimacy, which means the dynastic heritage of nations by individuals of particular families; the conservatism of ancient rights and constitutions; and the maintenance of legally instituted authority. These are good principles in themselves; necessary, or for the most part highly useful, to the stability of society; and the only fault to be found with the advocacy of them is when they are adduced as antagonistic to social progress and the natural expansion of popular rights in ages more enlightened than those in which their beginnings are to be traced. There are more good things capable of improvement than bad ones, and such are mostly the constitutions of nations.

In considering, first, briefly the relations of the government to the different states of which the empire is composed, the proclivity of Austrian policy hitherto has not only not been in the direction last spoken of, but unhappily too often towards the repression or taking away, as in the case of Hungary for the crime of its revolutionary outburst, what popular and legislative rights the citizens claimed still to possess.

These advantages, it is true, excited the

active jealousy of some of their fellow-subjects
in less favoured sections of the empire, and, so
far as any liberal institutions formed naturally
to a great extent the admiration and ideal
of others less favoured, might seem to justify
the Government in its subsequent treatment,
if the application of it had not been in the
wrong direction ; for, while after the successful suppression of the revolt the wiser course
would manifestly have been to diminish the
disparity between Hungarian and other semi-
national institutions, by elevating these to a
higher level with it, the object of its Austrian
rulers appeared to be, by utterly prostrating
the privileges of that troublesome and obstinate
state, to effect a general provincial uniformity
on the basis of certain other divisions possessing
no rights nor privileges whatever, save that of
unqualified dependence upon the central and
imperial authority,—an object analogous to
that sought in the religious sphere by means

of the *Concordat*. But in the development of this process of degradation all parties, it is needless to say, were discontented and disappointed : not only the Hungarians themselves, who keenly felt their reduced condition ; not only the other constituents of the Sclavonic race, who suffered proportionately in the disparagement of their head ; but also a large proportion of the Germanic element of the empire, which saw in the suppression of all legislative independence the death-blow to every free institution of a similar nature ; but, more than all, the Government itself—conscious of the failure of the *régime* adopted by it under the influence of advisers then fortunately no more, and which may be denoted simply by three words, Suppress, degrade, centralize —was discontented, disappointed, discomfited ; and under the pressure of considerations forced upon its attention during the closing events of the Italian war, pointing to the imminent

danger of a revolutionary coalition between the
so-called patriots of Hungary and Northern
Italy, came to the wise conclusion of altogether
altering the system upon which it had hitherto
acted; of conceding something to the spirit of
the times, and of widening and elevating the
foundation of imperial authority by the hitherto
unthought-of expedient of establishing popular
rights; and by respecting the natural dignity
of a people claiming the privilege of a share
in their own government. This so worthy
object, under the auspices of an enlightened
administration, has been successfully accomplished in the rehabilitation of the Old Imperial Council on a broader base than heretofore and with enlarged powers, consisting of
members partly nominated by the Crown,
partly elected as representatives of provinces;
the constitution of which important ruling
body not inaptly expresses at once the social
exigencies of the empire and its political posi-

tion between the dumb autocracy of the East
and the democratic garrulity of Western nations. Such an institution, elastic and doubtless improvable in various functions, is of the
utmost value in itself, and easily capable of
adaptation by other states in an approximate
political condition ; for it is from the comparative imperfection, and consequent expansibility,
of rude institutions, that their benefits result :
and no one but certain sages of the British
press—those who from the first have merely
ignored or libelled the Austrian Reichsrath—
would be capable of considering democratic
institutions suitable for that somewhat heterogeneous empire, the honest attempts of whose
rulers to walk in the ways of a constitutional
government were worthy of a more earnest and
more sympathetic welcome.

There is, indeed, no denying the fact that
the establishment of the Imperial Council has
entirely disarranged the bearings of the old

parties in the state, and their representatives abroad; the Austrian Government and the supporters of the new general system of popular representation and election now actually occupy the place of the van, the movement, the Liberal party; while the cause of Hungary has a selfish and domineering character attached to it which is repulsive to men of liberal sentiments, but who look below the surface of things. For what is the object, and what the grievance, of the Hungarians? Why should they be encouraged to insist upon an autonomy which results in a refusal to pay their just share in the general taxation of the country? What ground of superiority exists on their part, that their troops should not be liable to take service in all the varied districts of the empire along with those of the other nationalities? Does the fact of their having given a king to the empire three hundred years ago justify these presumptions and exemptions? Are the actual rights of living nations, their peace and prosperity, to be sacrificed with impunity to a pedantic and black-letter spirit of revolution which would imperil the well-being of millions, on account of the omission of certain cere- monies and formalities of coronation when the state was in the throes of a sanguinary con- vulsion, for which the complainants are them- selves responsible? And, finally, who are they for whom and by whom these demands and pretensions are set and kept on foot? Are they—as it will be, of course, supposed— the whole, or the vast majority, of the people of Hungary? Far from it. They are the Magyars, who do not form one-third of the population, the masses of whom are mostly a despised and powerless class.

The truth is, it is only in England, where free discussion is held to be of more importance than accurate judgment, that, amidst the mis- conceptions natural upon such matters, and the national foible of our day for encouraging rebellion, any enthusiasm is felt in favour of what are called Hungarian rights and liberties. The Germans generally, and even most of the Sclavonian populations around, would be astonished at the interest manifested on that theme by many eloquent orators and soul-stirring editors in this country; a fact which can only be accounted for from the former being a little better acquainted with the merits of the case than the sages of Fleet-street-cum-Finsbury and their followers. The Government of Austria is in general more liberal than the character and tendencies, in divers ways, of several of its constituent elements would lead an incautious observer to suppose; as may be noted in the instance of those interesting and romantic mountaineers of the Tyrol, who are actuated by a bitter and contemptuous hatred of all professing the Protestant form of faith; and whose animosities

the Imperial Government, in deference to the
just rights and natural feelings of others their
fellow-subjects, sternly and warrantably re-
strains. But the laws of Hungary, for the
reimposition of which so many publicists and
agitators assume the most frantic attitudes, or
utter the most delirious nonsense, are, many
of them—as in their persecuting spirit against
Jews and heretics—simply a disgrace to the
tolerant principles wisely prevailing in the
present age, and the enforcement of which
were tantamount to the reinstallation of a
mediæval savagery that would bear comparison
with the triumphs of the Inquisition. These,
be it understood, in defiance of the more humane, enlightened, and comprehensive system
of laws obtaining in the more strictly Germanic
states of the empire, are the standards of
Magyar legislation—the legislation of the dominant race in Hungary, and which those hereditary heroes are sadly solicitous to restore.

And why did the Hungarian rebellion fail? Because it was not supported by the masses of the population; and because it is undeniable that, in the face of Magyar domination and Magyar laws, the great body of the people sympathised, naturally and reasonably enough, rather with the. legions of the Czar, whom, though owing political allegiance to the Emperor of Austria, they, as Sclavonians, consider their natural head. Nor, on the other hand, need any more be said to account for that more than respectful distance at which the Court of Vienna placed itself immediately afterwards in relation to its imperial friend and saviour. Benefits may be as oppressive as wrongs.

It is much to be regretted that Hungary, in a territorial aspect the main element of the grandeur of Austria, should, in its social and political condition, prove a chief source also of her embarrassments; though these, perhaps, may not be so wholly insuperable as some well-known patriots would lead us to suppose; and who, constantly speaking of Switzerland as an independent state, maintain that, in certain contingencies, Hungary could at least do what Switzerland has done. But— apart from the natural reflection that, while one Switzerland may be for Europe a needful luxury, two might be a superfluity—to retain Hungary is a necessity for Austria, if she is to continue one of the dominant Powers of Europe; in other words, if the present equilibrium of races and forces is to subsist.

A few words will suffice for the treatment of the position and policy of Austria towards Poland, as far as they are directly concerned with each other. Her share in the first partition, bearing in mind the recent robbery of Silesia by Prussia, may be regarded as an act of political precaution, instances of which are to be found in the history of every country, and are rather to be justified by the event than by the means or the motive; for, as contributing to the division of the Sclavonic race, and subjecting it to the counterpoise of others, opposed under a common dominion to their individual predominance, the Western nations generally may be credited with the benefit actually derived from diminished danger and relief from alarm. The Sclavonic race, generally superstitious and unenquiring thralls of ecclesiastical, military, and imperial authority, must always be distrusted by the more enlightened but less socially cohesive races of Keltic and Teutonic origin, in whose mental characteristics may be numbered a propensity to reasoning, and, as a necessary accompaniment, a tendency to limit the exercise of irresponsible power. The normal state of the Sclavonic mind is favourable to despotism. Their political revolutions, which have never effected any improvement in their laws, have, after the Oriental manner, had principally in contemplation a personal change, not a constitutional advance. They have cushioned their rack, and padded their yoke; they cultivate the beautiful but servile arts ancillary to despotism; and are safe even from themselves; while united in imagination they remain divided in allegiance.

Now, as many honest and enthusiastic exiles, inoculated with ideas of French democracy, are fond of picturing to others an independent and united Hungary and Poland, each a living protest respectively against Russian and Austrian despotism, it may be well to contemplate for a moment this political theorem, and endeavour to ascertain, with what precision we can, the probable consequences. But if there be any truth or reliance to be placed in ethnology and its dependent sciences, we know that Hungary, Galicia, Bohemia, and other provinces now forming part of the Austrian empire, are occupied with a Sclave population;

and it may be certainly inferred that in case of a successful attempt on the part of Hungary to escape from Austrian rule, these members of the state above alluded to would cast in their lot with hers; while Austria herself would be reduced to the condition of a minor Power, dependent entirely on German elements. We then behold Hungary and Galicia; or the principal part of Austrian Poland, independent Powers, face to face with Russia. Could matters long remain so? Evidently, not a twelvemonth. The Poles of Galicia, akin to those of Russia, would, if in any more independent position, be an example and incitement to perpetual discontent on the part of the latter resident in Cracow, in Warsaw, and other districts of the Russian empire. War must follow; and the old feuds between the Great and Little Russians (that is, the Poles and Muscovites) would inevitably be revived. But, except on the supposition of a peaceable secession, of all things the most unlikely ; and granting, therefore, the existence of hostilities between Hungary and Russia, the result of these with the mass of the population of the former belligerent power, consisting of Slovaks and others who dislike while they submit to the Magyars, may readily be foreseen. Galicia would be ceded, by way of peace-offering, to Russia, who would thus acquire, on very easy terms—what she has notoriously long speculated upon—the Carpathians as a frontier. But her toleration of Hungarian independence would be simply parenthetical ; and all the nations of cognate origin would soon be glad to find themselves sitting in peace under the shadow of the great Sclavonian tree.

Let us then beware how far we assist the designs of doubtless well-meaning and eloquent exiles, who, burning with hostility against the authority which has expatriated them, are eager to propose or sanction any combination which appears to promise plentiful distress or embar-

rassment to the object of their hate, quite
regardless of the more general and ulterior
results to the highest civilization and most solid
liberties of Europe; whose only safeguard
against an inconceivable calamity consists in
the maintenance of the present politic, if somewhat complicated arrangements. Similar conclusions might be demonstrated, *mutatis mu-
tandis*, respecting the resuscitation of Poland,
and all the chimerical schemes and aspirations
in its behalf. There are many things which
when once lost can never be restored, whether
that loss has been produced by natural process
or by violence; nor as yet has the world seen
any instance of youth, or life, or national independence, twice flourishing in the same subject
in a condition of perfection.

Exposed to perils on all sides, these two
inferior states, whose independence is by many
thought so desirable, would, it is needless to
prove by any additional reasons, at the earliest

period possible, again fall irretrievably under the domination of one of the surrounding Powers ; for it is perfectly idle to suppose that those who are essentially of the same blood and language can operate as any check upon each other, unless allotted territorially to other Powers whose interests are not coincident ; and while at the same time among this sovereign fraternity of states, a certain proportion of territory, population, or physically productive power is a necessary condition. Finally, putting out of view as wholly untenable any proposal for a republican form of government, there remains, apart from the Imperial Houses, no central rallying point in either of these provinces in the shape of a traditional family, or any other, which could stand as the nucleus of an independent government.

There is every reason, however, now to believe that much of the selfish and arrogant pretensions of Hungary are being quietly abandoned, and that all classes of her population are being brought to perceive that, in the wise reformatory measure before named, conceded both to herself and sister provinces, a juster, more uniform, and more provident government, gradually granting to all its subjects a high equality of popular rights, may, by effectually conciliating its various nationalities, happily and permanently consolidate the whole.

The principle of nationalities is a force both conservative and destructive; one which in its milder form is productive of a wholesome tone among the various members of civilised society, but abundantly capable of exhibition as a ruinous and deadly irritant. It is a principle which, while indisputably one of the most powerful which actuate society, is, when operating in its pure and simple capacity, a barbarous principle; and, although the foundations of barbarism and civilization are common and concentric in human nature, it is only when modified and harmonized by the compression of surrounding influences and restricted by the interpenetration of rival interests, civil and political, that the stability and force requisite for the action of government can be combined and secured at the same time with the claims of a just and refined humanity.

War is the inevitable result of vicious and selfish policy. But whether the world would get on better without evil of any kind, is a problem which, while sternly set before us by the necessities of our nature, religion is always striving to solve individually, and law and diplomacy internationally and in the mass.

In order to penetrate the causes of the recent war in Italy, and fully appreciate the policy and position of Austria in relation to that country, the following considerations will, doubtless, have their due weight.

Power is in the north. The pressure of the

great dominating Powers of Europe is south-
wards and towards the sunny sea which bounds
the Continent in that direction, opening an
exit for the products, providing an adit for the
introduction of luxuries to the hardy and industrious inhabitants of the interior, and affording
their governments the opportunity of taking
part in other great events by the establishment
and employment of a suitable navy.

In possession of the fertile plains and popu-
lous cities of Venetia and Lombardy, ceded to
Austria finally by treaties conceived in a spirit
of hostile repression to France in the day of her
humiliation, and in the gradually but palpably
growing preponderance of Austrian influence
among the Italian States — of whose urban
population many always cherished the traditions, still troublesome, of ancient self-govern-
ment and republican independence—in these
ominous antecedents, overshadowing a number
of minor states, for ages the common arena

of French and German " difficulties," were paraded the ensigns of that bitter rivalry which fails never to mature, as we have seen, into active warfare ; and which, abruptly terminated for the present by the loss of one of those provinces, may even now any day be renewed on the principle of winning both or losing all.

To a nation like ourselves, isolated from all direct concern in the struggle, the results may be a matter of much indifference, and popular sympathies be with one or other belligerent as the conditions or interests of domestic policy may chance to decide ; but apart from the pretensions of the Court of Turin, which may be reserved for future consideration, and on certain grounds, social and moral, for the convenience and interest of vast masses of continental population, it is unreasonable to expect— it may be unwise to wish—to see Austria denuded of her remaining possessions on the north-east coast of the Adriatic. The command of the

Adriatic is traditionally attached to Venice;
and this Austria can never suffer to become the
subject of dispute. For it is to be observed
that, while the new kingdom of Italy has, com-
pared with its superficial area, an extensive
sea-coast and many most important harbours
both for purposes of naval armament and commercial intercourse, the vast empire of Austria
is mainly dependent for those objects upon
Venice and Trieste. To those who contend
that Austria ought in such case to be content
with Trieste alone, it is scarcely necessary to
reply that the upper part of the Adriatic is a
narrow sea, and that two ports, so situated,
each in possession of what must in all probability be considered for some time to come
as hostile powers, cannot, unless by miracle,
occupy such a position without ensuring perpetual collision between the respective navies—
in other words, chronic warfare between Austria
and Italy. There are others who, referring to

many fine ports and naval stations on the coast
and among the islands of Dalmatia, affirm
that, on the supposition above referred to,
Austria would find these suitable and sufficient;
but this is a mistake as far as regards commercial purposes, at least; for with the ex-
ception of the narrow strip of territory border-
ing the gulf which belongs to Austria, these
ports are the outlets to countries in which that
Power has either no interest, or the inhabitants
of which are totally destitute of those habits
and commodities which alone render such
places of importance. In addition, it must be
remembered that, as undoubtedly the highest
interests of England are involved in the
maintenance of Germany at large as a great
and powerful confederation by land and sea,
the preservation of Venice to Austria, as in
many respects the leading power of the Teutonic
race, is a matter of vital value not only to that
individual state, but to all nations of Germanic

origin or alliances. On the other hand, Genoa and Spezzia have those unsurpassed natural advantages adequate to all requirements of the honour and welfare of New Italy. The case of Venetia is certainly not one which invokes our sympathies on account of popular recollections associated with the enjoyment of past political rights, or even of good government, or amity with the sister states of Italy; for, however great and reasonable may be the native aversion to *Tedeschi* or *forestieri*, it is not easy to believe that the citizens of Venice, under the present rule, can look back with regret to the selfish, irresponsible oligarchy which expired in 1797; with one or two exceptions in its career, so much more interesting in poetry than illustrious in history. Our feelings in its favour are, therefore, connected with its aspirations for the future; and as the Austrian Government is rapidly assuming a constitutional character, and the province itself is by emigration and other causes becoming daily more German, it is reasonable to hope that, the causes of discontent being effectually diminished, the Venetians, by taking advantage of the political privileges offered by the advanced and liberal system under which they are now included, will ultimately recognise the beneficial results to be reciprocally secured by a more cordial union with the empire.

Bearing in remembrance the ruinous afflictions which she had suffered from 1795 to 1815, it is scarcely to be deemed a matter of wonderment that the policy of Austria, generally, since that period should have been directed by the most determined hostility to every measure or event savouring in the remotest degree of resemblance to democratic liberties ; but although grace must be conceded to the sentiments of a Government so situated, it is certain that this wild resistance to every impulse of democracy, and all desire for popular liberty, is as unwise as it is ineffectual. The conservative forces of society, the displacement of which the Austrian Government appears so much to have feared as the probable result of any administrative innovations, will, there is no doubt, even if driven from the political platform, sufficiently fortify themselves elsewhere under the friendly banners of religion, or education, or loyalty, or law. But, in the mean time, acting under the influence of the dread referred to, Austria, as the centre of European absolutism, having effected treaties with the Ducal Courts of Tuscany, Parma, and Modena, all allied to the Imperial family, constitutional governments were not only rendered impracticable, but the forcible suppression of every movement in favour of popular rights was guaranteed. In the States of the Church a similar object was secured by the military occupation of Bologna and other fortified towns, garrisoned by Austrian troops; and with Naples an express treaty was

concluded to prohibit the slightest manifestation of liberal or constitutional tendencies on
the part of either the King or the people. The
final outcome of all this was the war of 1859;
and the definitive abandonment by Austria,
as has been, or will be done by every state in
Europe, of the principle which till that period
formed the foundation of her policy.

On whatever side Austria is viewed, her difficulties undoubtedly appear to be great ; and
because, from her very complex system, she is
probably more sensitive to the least derangement in the condition of Europe than any other
State, it thus happens that, while the various
nationalities of which the empire is composed
she is compelled to employ to check each
other, so that in the *minimum* of their reciprocally irritant forces a sort of equilibrium is
effected, just sufficient to sustain the foundation
and action of Government, it is certain that,
from the variety of races and nations comprised

in her dominions, Austria has not only to be on
her guard against the centrifugal tendencies of
some of her constituent elements, but, several of
these being mostly in a state of chronic discontent—the natural consequence of her hitherto
neglected legislation, or the centralizing system
so long substituted for it—she is at all times
perhaps less absolutely secure than her jealous
and powerful neighbours, either more or less
socially advanced, and all more politically
uniform in their internal constitutions, who
surround her confines.

In the mean time, the alleged ingratitude of
Austria to Russia, after the gratuitous suppression by the latter of the Hungarian revolt,
shown in her vacillation and final neutrality,
so embarrassing to the Emperor Nicholas, during
the war on the Danube and in the Crimea, has
effected a wholesome coolness between the two
Powers, an estrangement indeed between the
two peoples, which it is to be hoped no abortive

attempts at insurrection, though concealed under heaps of *immortelles* and the disguise of prayers intoned before a senseless statue, by alarming their united interests, may altogether remove. On the other hand, there can be no doubt that the presumptive interests of these governments, resting mostly on the unreasoning instinct of fidelity in the people to their rulers, instead of any rational attachment to moral principles or social aims, supply sufficient motives for their reunion, whenever it can be effected at the expense of a common victim; for which position, the Principalities, it was thought, by reason of their more liberal institutions, were not unlikely involuntarily to qualify themselves. But the state of political society in Europe at the present time, it must be confessed, is such, that both the elements of power and the bases of calculation are disordered and inverted or invalidated.

Although therefore, apart from Italy, where

her star has suffered detriment, Austria has long ceased to be regarded as an aggressive Power, yet in certain contingencies dependent on the Turkish question, and if no disruption be precipitated by the attempted foundation of a new Roumaic dominion, her claims upon the Christian populations of Servia, Bosnia, Bulgaria, and other parts of European Turkey, would to many of them appear quite equal in point of attraction to those upon which Russia calculates for the advancement of her own designs. On the borders of the Ottoman empire, therefore, no less than on the Drave and the Danube, Austria has to contend against the same rival striving for the same object. To divide the Danube between them as the common highway and part boundary of the two empires is probably the secret and not ill-judged design of these Powers; for there can be no doubt that, if exclusively under their control as anticipated, it might and would be greatly improved as a medium of commercial intercourse between the western and eastern portions of Europe, and even between Europe and Asia.

In spite of the financial embarrassments too frequent in Austria, and maugre the sad predictions of many ill-disposed friends, her ruin is not yet even probable. The resources of the empire are almost boundless; and these must be far more seriously encroached upon than they have been during the last fifty years—a period of unparalleled trial—before insolvency can be pronounced. Agriculture is improving; her production suffices for her own consumption; her exports are increasing: the area of her deficiencies is diminishing; manufactures are extending; neither famine nor penury is known among the people. Nor is the army that monstrous incubus upon the energies and resources of the state which has been supposed. Military service in these great Continental states being compulsory, it must be remembered that where the habits of life are simple, and the mass of the people uninstructed, provisions plentiful, labour cheap, and manufacturing and commercial enterprise scarce or restricted, the army becomes an administrative establishment into which the youth of the country enter as into a provident institution. Where military service and agriculture are the ruling if not all-inclusive ideas of the subject, the army is used by the Government as the common school of such physical and moral discipline as it considers desirable for the many, and as the main organ for the diffusion of loyalty to the Crown and the propagation of a spirit of reciprocal forbearance among the various classes and populations of the empire. Among these it forms the natural resource of thousands to whom compulsory service is a relief, as they would probably be otherwise without remunerative employment during the most active period of their lives.

PRUSSIA.

PRUSSIA.

PRUSSIA, as the leading Protestant Power on the Continent, is in this respect, as in so many others, the rival of absolute and faithful Austria. The Prussian people are not noted for a vital and profound sense of dogmatic religion. Many degrees, doubtless, of mental culture and religious orthodoxy are to be found between the enlightened classes, denizens of the universities and capital cities, and the superstitious who await with anxiety the next exposure of the Holy Coat at Trèves. The national mind, however, generally, and of the cultivated classes especially, is marked by a speculative, argumentative, and philosophical tendency. Tolerant almost to a fault, and temperate nearly to excess, their creed is nullified neither by a gloomy egotism nor a fervid fanaticism. The Protestant bishopric of Jerusalem, which Prussia and Great Britain united to establish, the diocese of which precisely coincides with the periphery of the episcopal residence, recommended itself to the popular sympathies as a species of spiritual knighthood, and an almost allegorical crusade, which, whatever effect it might produce upon Paynim incredulity, was certainly a proof that modern Germans knew better what was consistent with the genius of Christianity than our Cœur-de-Lion and his followers, or than their own Teutonic knighthood, the pious slaughterers of the Borussians.

The form of government, originally and till recently a pure autocracy, having been at the first foundation of the kingdom imposed upon the people, and not having, as in early constitutional states, grown from them, the intermediate power of the state is found to be the army, which, being necessary and co-extensive with the population, partakes of the character of a civil as well as military institution. This service, comprising the youth and enthusiasm of the entire nation, is mostly, for the time being, the simple reflex of royal and official absolutism. On leaving the army, if no more lucrative occupation presents itself to the choice of the young soldier, derived from private means or family influence, he is accounted most deserving who is most loyal; every degree downwards of subserviency standing for as many upwards of promotion in the civil service of the state to which he is now attached.

Except in the capital and a few large towns, the sentiment of political rights for the people does not deeply influence the national mind. The cultivation and laudation of freedom, indeed, as a theme, is pursued with ardour at the universities principally. If the indulgence

of a theory has not realized more tangible results, it is, probably, that they are not required;
for among a people where there is no lack of
employment, nor its due reward, settled laws
justly administered, education encouraged, a
religion of their own choice, and conscience un-
constrained, the degree of political power which
they may claim as a class is a matter not of
indifference, but of less importance and of
doubtful advantage. The people may, in this
sense, have too much power to use it for their
own good, as is invariably the case with demo-
cracies. The highest results of civilization are
found not in endowing with uniform power the
masses, but with varied privileges the great co-
ordinate classes of society. Political liberty
implies with us the unlimited right of public
meeting, free discussion by tongue and pen,
representative institutions, parliamentary control over taxation and the application of the
finances of the state; but not to every nation

are these powers indispensable. And if with some the cultivation and exercise of the deeper capacities of our nature, philosophical habits of mind, the graceful studies and refined achievements of art, have more of vital attraction than with ourselves, each may be considered to possess equal advantages.

With a government of autocratic origin and habits, supported by a highly conservative aristocracy, in favour of alliance and assimilation to Russia, rather than any more westward Power; and with a bureaucratic administration, —which, as every institution has a better and a worse side, may be said to signify in the latter sense the popular element in a state of social subornation and political perjury, constrained to bear witness in favour of superior authority,— territorial influence may be expected to predominate, as it does, even in many properly public proceedings, and forming naturally the great reserve of the arbitrary authority of the

Crown. A considerable enlargement, nevertheless, in late years, of civil liberties has been fairly won by the people, in the minds of whose leaders and teachers England and her institutions are the great and guiding exemplar. As a national consequence, the forms of a constitutional monarchy, and the establishment of an Upper and Lower House, have given Prussia a pre-eminence as the head and patron of free discussion, political as well as philosophical, which men of liberal views in all countries are naturally inclined to approve; and from which it is hoped the principle of the adoption of representative institutions is destined to attain a wider range than it has yet done on the continent of Europe.

With all this, whether as a corollary from foregoing conditions, or as a characteristic of pure Teutonic mind, the most remarkable features of Prussian policy, as apparent in its external relations, are inconsistency and indecision. When any question requiring co-operative solution is submitted to the consideration of her government, while others are prompt and energetic, authoritative or obstinate, Prussia is for the most part vacillatory. Not to go back to any remote period, it is sufficient to refer to her conduct in relation to France, from the anti-republican manifesto of Pilnitz, in 1791, to her projected invasion of that country in 1793, in which a retreat was the only thing accomplished; to her acceptance, in 1794, of a British subsidy in support of war; to the treaty of Basle, the year following, by which she as treacherously secured the advantages of peace; to her subsequent adhesion to the northern maritime confederacy and attack upon British interests at the moment that Power was making sacrifices and exceptions in her favour; her invasion of Hanover in compliance with the arrogant demands of France in 1806; her rupture immediately afterwards with that

Power, and her renewed subservience, after defeat, to Napoleon, as manifested in the toleration of the Berlin decrees and in the treaty of Tilsit; her support of the Russian invasion in 1812; and, finally, in 1813, the initiation by the Prussian government of that great alliance against the despot her own vacillation and servility had contributed so grossly to aggrandise.

Internally her conduct has been almost equally inconsistent, though due allowance must always be conceded to the ill-directed and extravagant course of popular illusion and national ambition, as may be noted in her when, after passing through a period of pure autocracy, the reactionary effect of the first French Revolution, as a member of the Holy Alliance and one of the great despotic triad of the North, in 1846 she was seized with the natural desire for constitutional institutions; her tendencies being rationally developed among all classes, and honourably encouraged by the king, when the unhappy outbreak of the French introduced also into Prussia a degree of democratic violence and unjust assumption on the part of both sovereign and people which, at first directed unitedly against other and external objects, ultimately, as might be expected, issued in a collision between themselves. In this struggle the sovereign having succeeded, though only by open duplicity, in securing the safety of those social institutions which all classes are interested in preserving, at any cost, against the onslaught of turbulent and momentarily demented myriads, subsequent reflection induced the former, fortified by the support of the more judicious section of his subjects, himself to abandon, and suppress in others as far as he could, those wild and lawless schemes of absorption and annexation which formed so long the day-dreams of dyspeptic editors, and the mental cloudland of so many beardless patriots. Ultimately, it is

E

gratifying to find that the sober and practical attractions of a limited constitutional monarchy have proved sufficient to secure the political devotion of the citizens, and preclude the prospect, each successively threatening, and both alike to be dreaded, of a return to anarchy or to absolutism.

In 1854-55, and during the whole of the negotiations previous to the war in the Crimea, as well as in the actual hostilities, Prussia held aloof with Austria both from Russia and the Allies, apparently bent upon embarrassing, rather than assisting, either party; although, in this instance, being but remotely connected with the contest, its causes, and its consequences, her motives for non-interference, coupled with dynastic alliance and the pacific predilections of the king, are sufficiently obvious. In 1859 she waited till Austria had lost her finest province before adopting any decisive measure; and in 1860, on the question of Savoy, said nothing till it was too late. She then spoke out very emphatically.

As it is frequently difficult, nevertheless, to decide whether reluctance to engage in hostilities, or even to adopt bold measures, arises from sluggishness or astuteness, the backwardness of Prussia in the matter of the Italian war may be reasonably well accounted for on the principle, perfectly understood in Germany, which may be thus formulated: any positive loss to Austria is at least a negative gain to Prussia; there being no possibility of the converse ever proving true. The latter, it was thus foreseen, would look with complacency on the loss by her rival of those possessions beyond the Alps the absence of which tended to leave both upon terms of more equality.

That there is reason to fear Prussia will almost always prove an unsafe or unreliable ally may be inferred from the fact that, while the tendency of her constitutionally inclined

population is, of course, to the friendship
and support of liberal governments, theories,
and measures of administration foreign and
domestic, her active advocacy or support of
such is always liable to be paralysed, at marked
political crises and doubtful contingencies of
peace or war, by certain overwhelming exigencies in two most important quarters connected simply with territorial considerations.
If Austria and Russia at any juncture combine
in an offensive attitude, Prussia must eventually join them or remain neuter. While these
are at variance, she is comparatively free.
But under no circumstances can Prussia afford
to enter into actual hostilities with Russia or
with Austria unless one of these is her ally.

Again, in regard to the Rhenish Provinces,
her position, in the event of a war with France,
is such as to necessitate naturally the utmost
degree of anxiety. To these considerations
may partly be ascribed her vacillating policy

at different times. But the fact remains. Prussia is a variable star, and only nominally of the first magnitude. Her interests, however, are identical with those of Austria in precluding the further insidious advances of Russia towards the heart of Europe ; and since both powers have been relieved by the death of the late Czar from the oppressive tutelage of that imperial head, a more dignified and independent course of action may not unreasonably be looked for.

Identical also are the interests of all three on one vital point, viz., in repressing—however harsh it may appear to uninterested spectators, if such there be—any manifestation of Polish nationality. In fact, it is their equal and united interest so to balance and modify their treatment of that people that, under their respective governments, not one of them—neither Austrian Poland, Russian Poland, nor Prussian Poland—may have greater reason than another to complain or to congratulate itself. Poland, therefore, although as a nationality extinct, remains, among the Powers which divided it, the pivot of their peculiar international policy.

The opinion has been entertained that the circumstance most to be regretted—since the division is irremediable—is the disproportion of the allotments; for while Russia has seized two-thirds of the territory, the remaining third only has been subdivided between Austria and Prussia; and various reasons could doubtless be adduced why it might have been better had the proportions been reversed, or the distribution been, at least, more equal. In favour of it, it can only be said that, in relation to the other states, the repressive power of Russia is of course proportionally greater; and that, if the act were, as its promoters contended, for the advantage of the European system, agreeable to the peace and progress of society and the more general security of order and civilization, the arrangement finally adopted is sufficiently capable of justification.

Neither carelessly nor callously, the writer would remark, is this term justification used while speaking of the dismemberment of a once powerful and independent state ; but, in truth, the disordered condition of Poland, owing to the internal factions of its own mercenary, tyrannical aristocracy, and the disorganization effected by the unjust interference of Charles XII., the baneful effects of which were palpable for more than half a century ; added to the danger of French intervention, believed to be imminent by those Powers in more immediate contact with the royal republic—a mass of political contradictions and anomalies—rendered England and the rest of Europe somewhat indifferent to its fate; assured, moreover, as the judicious statesmen of every country must have been, that, even were it parcelled out among its more potent neighbours, the condition of the great masses of the Polish people could not possibly be deteriorated by their incorporation with any regular government, however despotic, but, in all probability, be sensibly improved; and, conclusively, that since its fall appeared no less than inevitable, it were safer for all, in regard to future contingencies, that so formidable a prize should be distributed among a plurality of competitors than permitted solely to aggrandize one. Thus a measure apparently and theoretically unjust proved to be practically wise, and one in which both distant spectators and immediate actors were almost equally interested and benefited. For so long as Poland stood by its absurd constitution—in which the veto of a single noble, however treacherous or mercenary might be his vote, sufficed to nullify the unanimous resolutions of successive senates—in which, too, by reason of its elective sovereignty, the seat of regal faction and imperial intrigues, and while the inability of the law to provide for the succession during the life of the actual wearer of the crown secured a constantly recurring quantity of anarchy and corruption, its royal rivals and its vast and ill-regulated population rendered it to the rest of Europe a source of universal and perpetual peril. The further consideration that, while Poland remained even doubtfully an independent and united Power, there only lacked a crowned leader of military genius and energetic character, and the advent of a suitable opportunity, to jeopardize or embarrass, or, at all events, compel to a state of perpetual armed vigilance, the surrounding Governments, furnished, doubtless, another weighty and decisive argument for the tripartition ; while the distrust entertained by the Courts of Russia and Austria in relation to the ambitious views and victorious arms of Prussia, in connexion with

other causes recorded in history or only half
concealed in private memoirs, amply account
for the different proportions of the allotment.
While, therefore, for the removal of this cause
of general uneasiness to Europe, civilized society
is paradoxically indebted to the rapacity of
Russia and Austria, it is not a little, perhaps,
owing to the determination of the Prussian
King to render his own state, by military
organization and the extension of his dominions, a co-ordinate member of the first rank
of continental monarchies.

The Westphalian provinces, separated by a
land-strait from the bulk of the kingdom and
inhabited almost wholly by a Roman Catholic
population, form, from their heterogeneous
character in position, race, and religion, eminently the weak point of Prussia; for, in the
event of any convulsion or considerable superficial change in the conditions of European
society, while there is every probability that

certain of the intermediate states would attach themselves, by the laws of social attraction, to the greater mass of their Protestant brethren near at hand, so, by the operation of similar causes, the inhabitants of these provinces have a tendency to gravitate politically in the direction of the two most liberal Roman Catholic Powers of the Continent. But, at the same time, it is a proof of shortsightedness on the part of agitators to encourage or embitter reflection upon such topics. Interest, more effectually than religion, teaches charity to the dominant majority; and there is little doubt that in this reciprocal subordination of Protestant to Roman Catholic and Roman Catholic to Protestant rulers, humanity and liberty are on the whole gainers.

Distinguished by a loyal, enthusiastic, and concentrative population, even those outside her borders being actuated by what may be termed centripetal tendencies, it is in her relations with the minor states of Germany that Prussia appears in her most interesting and important aspect; but with what degree of consistency or sincerity she has assumed the championship of Germanic nationality, Germanic unity, and constitutional liberty, has yet to be assayed; a deeper inquiry even may be preferred to ascertain how far the principles of popular control, the practice of free assembly, and the enjoyment of unrestricted discussion, essential to the integrity of constitutional government, are compatible with the habits of a population taught to be soldiers before acquiring the rights of civil life, and what may be the value of these conditions when co-operative and when opposed, qualified by the antecedents of a state so long recognisable as a mere stratocracy.

Having, however, by means of this assumption, and the preponderating influence accruing from her position in the Commercial Customs

Union, as steward and dispenser of the revenues of divers petty States of the Confederation—a position which, with the Union itself, Austria, as might be anticipated, has always selfishly, stedfastly, and vainly opposed—acquired a commanding grasp over various political contingencies which, while awakening the fears of some, stimulate in a high degree the expectant patriotism of not only her own subjects, but a numerous *clientèle* on all sides of her actual dominions, the intentions of our self-styled "Sword of Germany" at any future crisis may fairly be estimated by the supposed gravity, in any particular direction, of her interests.

So long as Prussia was an aggressive Power in any other quarter than eastwards, it was the interest of western Europe generally, and England in especial, to support Austria, as in her resistance under Maria Theresa to the encroachments of the Prussian monarch, on account of his dominions being conterminous with those of Hanover,

in the prosperity and independence of which
England was, of course, vitally concerned. But
of all the Powers of Europe, the one which, at
the present moment, gives most unmistakable
evidence of ambitious designs is Prussia; and
though the tendency of the territorial and aristocratic element of Prussian society is towards
the adoption of an exclusive and self-isolating
policy, yet the policy of annexation, or the
unification of Germany, is without doubt more
popular both in ministerial circles and in democratic discourses. The result in such case
would be that Prussia would have, as it is
wished, a more compact domain and a more
decided policy; no longer "halting betwixt
two opinions," a character so singularly sym-
bolised by her territorial configuration; and
perhaps an absolutism more defensible because
possibly necessary.

GERMANY

AND

SCANDINAVIA.

GERMANY

AND

SCANDINAVIA.

———◆◇◆———

SCATTERED like the asteroids between the orbits of Mars and Jupiter, lie, betwixt the borders of France and those larger and ulterior bodies of our political system situated in the northern and eastern quarters of Europe, the many irregular and fragmentary statelets of Germany. Manifold are their tendencies, their interests discordant, their characteristics conflicting, no less than their apparent destinies.

To enter into a minute estimate of these and their several bearings upon each other, in reference to the greater states and to the general

F

scheme or figure of continental politics, is fortunately not necessary for the general reader; although, as regards German policy in its exclusive sense, it would be found as requisite to study them as for the mathematician to master the intervening text between any remotely successive problems of Euclid. It will obviously be sufficient to suggest a few considerations connected with the present state of affairs to exhibit a specimen of the attractive complications which beset the mind of the observer in noting accurately the curious configurations of German policy.

The Germanic Confederation, of which all these states are sovereign members, was naturally disposed, politically intended to be, and still to a large extent undoubtedly is, a great central conservative Power, calculated to preserve the peace of Europe from, on the one hand, the outbreaks of democracy, and, on the other, from the inroads of despotism. This laudable object the German people generally have pretty faithfully sought; and the states conjointly, in the constitution of their Diet, the apportionment of its functions, and the regulation of its powers, may be said to have secured the perfection of political conservatism. Unhappily, the tendency of all mortal perfection is to decline; and with the advance of popular intelligence and the expansion of the sphere of public opinion, the legislative deficiencies of the Diet have become more apparent, and its executive authority less capable of enforcement, defiance or neglect of which among both the stronger and weaker members seems likely to become soon the sole symbol of unanimity.

The question of the political hegemony of the Confederation, disputed between Austria and Prussia, or rather by their literary champions, chiefly at present in the speculations of the press or the declamations of university orators, and in which, as there is no possibility of agree-

ment, all arguments have equal force, nevertheless excites considerable interest in thoughtful
minds, and enlists their sympathies accordingly
as they are attracted by historical or progressive associations; for to this contested position Austria would naturally lay claim as the
first of German and imperial Powers, and as
hers by heirship of the ancient empire; but
Prussia, from rivalry with Austria, by right of
a younger strength, superior enlightenment and
intelligence, and popular support. This question, which in its more practical bearing on the
military leadership of the Confederation in
time of war, occupies not unfrequently the field
of constitutional discussion, the minor kingdoms
and some less considerable principalities treat
with a sagacious modesty which cannot be too
much admired; contending that, as they cannot
presume to decide between such high pretensions
as those put forward by the grand competitors
before named, the right might more justly and

without any suspicion of sinister designs be relegated to themselves, whose interests, as collectively the weaker party, whether considered in relation to a possible enemy, external or internal, to the Confederation, are most vitally involved; and the plea appears reasonable, but is no nearer adoption, it is to be feared, on that account.

The present dualism, as it is called, of Germany, is regarded by some, those especially of the national Verein party, as prejudicial to the honour and interests of the nation; though it is somewhat difficult to an unexalted mind to discover in what the detriment consists. Others would be content with merely enlarging the boundaries of the two great primary Powers by the aggregation to each respectively of a number of lesser states, so as to divide the whole Teutonic territory into a Northern and Southern Germany; but when it is considered that the population of many of these minor states, naturally intelligent and inclined to intellectual studies, refined by the influence of education and the arts, distinguished by simple habits and domestic virtues, with few burdens and fewer responsibilities, are amongst the best-conducted and happiest in Europe or the world, the benefit to be derived from the projected disarrangement of the present order of things appears to be at least highly problematical.

The honour of a country, it may be conceded, if not of a material, is far from being of an insubstantial or unimportant character; and it is really found that one at least of the principal grievances which the small states have to complain of under the actual system is that, in consequence of the inertness and incapacity of the Diet to assert its authority, their subjects are unable in foreign countries or at sea to vindicate their dignity when insulted, or when injured to obtain redress.

An emigrant from Schwartzburg-Rodolstadt in the aqueous wilds of Paraguay, or a scientific traveller from Kniphausen among the saline sands of Independent Tartary, may be robbed or maltreated, it is urged, with impunity, while neither the empire of Austria nor the kingdom of Prussia will man a paltry squadron or levy one battalion in his behalf. Such sweeping conclusions drawn from palpable and only possible exceptions it is unnecessary to combat : but the idea of an united Germany and a national flag appears to have taken root in the mind of the nation; and one thing is certain, that it is vain to contend against the general tendencies of the times, whether for good or for evil, either in social or political matters.

The great question indeed of the future. upon which, as usual, enthusiasm is universal, but judgment inexact, is that of the reconsolidation, under more popular conditions, of a

German empire. Although this is manifestly a project of that doubtful nature that, while it might by bare possibility be achieved by peaceful means, such as would be implied in the dissolution by the Diet of its own authority, and the re-election on a more popular basis of a common parliament at Frankfort or elsewhere, which should not be devoted exclusively to the consideration of petty dynastic intérests, but the broad measures of national utility, and the general improvement of society in its most important aspects, yet it might on the other hand require or occasion a convulsion similar to that experienced by Europe at the close of the last and commencement of the present century. Were it only a question of the sword, the settlement might be simple enough in nature, though in all probability more cruelly protracted in the process of solution than may be anticipated. But the inquiry naturally emerges, of what advantage would such a change be to European interests generally, or to Germany and the German people themselves?

And here, taking the hypothesis of a third independent Power, the difficulties in which the subject is involved, though sensible only at the present moment to a deliberative judgment, would at the most unhappy and unthought-of junctures, infallibly obtrude themselves. It is undoubtedly the right and the duty of a people to constitute itself under such conditions as to secure peace, prosperity, and safety at home, and respect abroad. Setting aside, therefore, as irrelevant, the dissatisfaction with which France who forcibly dissolved the former empire, and Russia who selfishly sanctioned the fact, would naturally regard the foundation of another, and the introduction of a new Power into Europe, while the consent of England might be fairly assumed as probable, there is no question but that from its nearest neighbours, and its national kindred in the

first degree, that is from both Austria and
Prussia, it would be met with a decided and
strenuous opposition. But if, in spite of those
troubles in Hungary and in Poland which
might at such a crisis be safely calculated upon,
the project as a whole, and in its main object,
were to miscarry and end in a double partition
between Austria and Prussia, as appears the
most probable issue of the plan, then the
dualism already alluded to would be permanently and in all likelihood beneficially established. Beneficially, of course, supposing the
maintenance and growth in each dominion of
representative institutions and responsible governments, not to speak of prudent parliaments. For, how imprudently a representative
assembly, popularly elected, can act, and
honestly, as it were, betray the people who
delegated them, is notably evident in the
elevation by the Frankfort Parliament in 1849
of an Austrian Archduke, though believed to

be liberally inclined, as the administrator of the embryo empire then in contemplation. A more directly suicidal step was never taken by even a democratic congress. The jealousy of Prussia and the contempt of the country insured its downfall.

Throughout this cluster of states, traversed from one point to the other, and to opposite extremes, by Gallic antipathies and democratic sympathies, by the hopes and fears of a progressive society, by the sense of insecurity inseparable to the possession of power from all innovation however reasonable or imperative; and the frequent antagonism arising from constitutional inclinations on the part of the people to the somewhat despotic predilections of the ruling powers, encouraged occasionally, if not originally instigated, by foreign corruption through the medium of family and other influences; the diverse religious prejudices of various states, and their voluntary or com-

pulsory toleration of each other's peculiarities,
—these form a sample of those important
questions which agitate or concentrate the
public mind, which in the flow and reflow of
popular opinion can only be viewed as indicative of a transitionary or preparatory state,
the probable results of which it is not easy to
define nor desirable to attempt.

As at present constituted, the weight of Germany is thrown into the scale of Conservatism;
and with the example of France before her,
and her own long-extended historical recollections, and with the perils of Panslavism and the
contingent perturbations of a resuscitated Poland, and an ignorant, hostile, or selfish Sclave
population on all sides of her, it is difficult to
wish it otherwise. That the Germans, as a
people, are desirous and deserving of a greater
amount of political liberty, freedom of speech,
freedom of the press, freedom of action in state
affairs, than they at present enjoy, is certain;

nor is there any recklessness or ferocity or
fanaticism in their character in any such degree
as to suggest the fear that the innovations they
contemplate would be attended with consequences fatal to others or prejudicial to themselves. It is greatly to be hoped that the
views of extreme democratic parties may not
be allowed to prevail; and that if possible—
former failure notwithstanding — the existing
machinery of legislation connected with the
functions of the Diet should be utilized; that
the overwhelming and antagonistic influence
of Austria and Prussia should be altogether
removed from the Confederation; that a uniform principle of popular franchise and representation should be adopted, as well as of
customs, taxes, rates, tolls, and other objects
of fiscal regulation, in addition to the rights
of independency secured to each state, and in
analogy with the proportions of military obliga-
tion and organization already established by
the central authority.

With these and other similar conditions it might be possible to effect the unification of Germany, considered as comprising the minor states distinguished from the two larger ones. A division even between these, though necessarily extending, in some measure, and intensifying the existing antagonism between them, might possibly prove beneficial or satisfactory on the whole, as securing to each individual Teuton, within their respective territories, a share, however atomic, in the rights and dignities of a powerful Fatherland. And such is apparently the tendency of popular opinion, that Dualism promises to be the destiny of Germany. In its present subdivided state, a discriminating glance at some of the more notable, though minor, members of the Confederation, their characteristics, position, and interests, may be not useless in the attempt to form a brief and rapid estimate of the internal policy of the Teutonic Governments.

Hanover, it is obvious, occupies, with regard

to Prussia, a peculiar and perilous position. In this respect the policy of Prussia was formerly—*i. e.* before the separation of Hanover from the British Crown—of more apparent importance in a territorial point of view to England than at present; and though it is not impossible that in any case of peril occurring to Hanover, in connexion with its neighbours, from external sources, a regard to ancient connexions and the obligations of treaties— which, it is needless to add, are constructed in express terms to endure for ever—might induce Great Britain to interpose in its favour, either by arms or diplomacy, yet it is certain that among our own statesmen a growing indifference to Hanoverian difficulties may be noted, arising from the arbitrary and reactionary tendencies of its government, too often in direct opposition to the wishes and requirements of an educated and enlightened population; which in this state and in certain neighbouring duchies feel, it is suspected, a somewhat dangerous confidence in the future liberality of Prussia.   Yet it must be confessed that the repulsion which the Hanoverian Government, supported by a very considerable party, feels towards Prussia and the ambitious views entertained by that Power, is readily to be conceived and only natural ; for in the history of the world there are but few independent states who have chosen to play the part of voluntary victims for the good of others, especially their inferiors in position.   The dominions of Hanover, with its maritime advantages, and other independent territories, intervening between the provinces of Westphalia and those of Prussia proper, give rise, it is clear, in the minds of Prussian statesmen, to a great temptation, which in these days, when subjects vote away their kings with as little ceremony as formerly kings disposed of their subjects, might present, probably, no very astounding obstacle to a Government accustomed to play a leading part in popular elections, and give due and imposing effect to democratic demonstrations; but to impartial observers of such a movement it would appear most unwise should the population so transferring themselves, in obedience to a clamour for theoretic unity, neglect very scrupulously to exact, from a Government thus increasing its territory and power, efficient guarantees for the parallel extension of civil liberties. Otherwise, indeed—and in the excitement attending national crises such things are frequently lost sight of—but little might be gained for which the friends of freedom would have reason to rejoice. This expectant attitude, however, to which allusion has just been made, on the part of various minor states, Prussia— whose future it is more easy to conceive than safe to foretell—naturally encourages; and it is an attitude of which other more strictly constitutional states, whose position is better secured, or thought so to be, might more freely and hopefully approve, could any firm reliance be placed upon the validity of institutions nominally asserting the principle of popular control over the Government in a state so situated as is Prussia in respect to her outward relations; and where, within, the entire population being compulsory conscripts, the one grand reality of the social system is the army. But the required security is felt to be wanting.

Bavaria, principally Roman Catholic, from proximity of position, royal alliances, trading, and other interests, mostly follows the lead of Austria. Though nominally a constitutional monarchy, its political action is so checked and overruled by the Diet that the wholesome inclinations of the people are in a great degree nullified.

Saxony—Lutheran Protestant as regards the majority of the population, but the reigning family, the original protectors of Luther, now

Roman Catholic—is theoretically a democratic state in the shape of a constitutional monarchy, but practically a bureaucracy in the hands of the sovereign; while the democratic party, therefore, sympathises mostly with Prussia, the party of independence, headed by royalty, inclines towards Austrian policy.

Wirtemburg—also for the most part Roman Catholic, and a constitutional state—adopts a policy more independent in some respects than the other minor monarchies; and its king may be considered as the head of that party, gradually assuming more importance, composed for the purpose of asserting the dignity of these greater mediocrities of the Germanic system; and this course is doubtless partly traceable to the position of Wirtemburg with regard to her western neighbour.

The Duchy of Baden has Chambers, and is, nominally at least, a constitutional state. The Duchies of Brunswick identify their interests with those of Hanover. To the Mecklenburgs Prussia has a reversionary claim. To the same power the Duke of Saxe Coburg has, with a sublime confidence, intrusted the entire control of the military forces of his state, in such a manner as to induce the belief that that measure implies a prejudgment on his part, at least, of the military leadership of Germany before referred to.

The question of a fleet to an inland people, like most of the members of the Germanic Confederation, would appear at the first glance to be of singularly small importance, or even of remote probability of occurrence; but, as recently the National Unionists have laid the foundations of a navy by improvising a flag, and commenced in earnest a penny subscription for a military marine, consisting, or to consist, of a hundred gunboats or more, which are destined to immortalise the maritime renown of the miner and the mountaineer in

Saxony, Wirtemburg, and a number of petty principalities which Nature has sedulously secluded from all idea of the sea, it is not improbable that the shallow ports of the Southern Baltic may shortly witness, under the command of Prussian and pro-Prussian admirals, a respectable and efficient flotilla, the employment of which supplies, at least, another foregone conclusion as to the naval leadership of Germany.

The dispute involved in the relations of Germany through Holstein with Denmark is peculiar and important, not only in the bearings indicated, but through a much wider range. Though asserted to be a simple question by ex-amnestied writers of high revolutionary rank, who, like the Magyars, with ostentatious inconsistency, are always appealing to ancient authority, and always endeavouring to overthrow it, there is, probably, no matter of political debate which precipitates in its train so many and considerable interests connected with the equilibrium of rival states, the laws of nations, the rights of races, their fears and aspirations.

This duchy and its half-sister, the most important fraction of the Danish dominions in Europe, was from 1848 to '51 the scene of a civil war instigated by the National party in Germany, and, of course, the Prussian Government—who, with its king and people, unwisely and criminally consented to render themselves the organ and exponent of that movement. But though the German Parliament and the Prussian people showed neither reluctance in inciting rebellion, nor hesitation in attacking the gigantic power of Denmark, yet at this moment Russia interfered with a forbidding and somewhat disquieting attitude, warranted, as she asserts, by the contingent succession of the Czars to the dukedom of Holstein—an assertion which is, unfortunately, too true.

Prussia and Germany are naturally in want of a deep-sea harbour, which is to be found at Kiel. Russia would not let the shadow of a chance slip by, which might give her a station on the German Ocean. Austria sent troops to the support of the King of Denmark, and as earnest of opposition to the ambitious policy of Prussia. Sweden is interested in confining Russia to the ports of the Baltic; and it was doubtless in the face of possible complications of the most serious character that Prussia finally retreated, not without military discomfiture, from the Holstein contest. It is urged by the National Unionists that, were the Duchies, or even Holstein only, incorporated with Germany, the strongest possible bar would thus be presented to the hostile advance of Russia; but the peculiar position of the Danish possessions is such that, unless Europe is prepared remorselessly to sacrifice Denmark as an entirety, she must be permitted to hold as her own the whole of the peninsula and islands of which her states are composed. Higher considerations, as they may be justly deemed in a certain sense, those of race, religion, and language, have occasionally, in all ages of the world, but righteously and beneficially, been made to yield to the more imperious obligations of natural position. And if the German nation, whether in its present merely federal form, or in that of the hoped-for Germany of the future, honourably and disinterestedly advocate the principles which they profess, and which surely imply those of good policy and humanity, it is certain they could, under even the untoward circumstances alluded to, as a friendly Power, afford equal support to that which they boast of being able to furnish were the disputed provinces in their actual possession.

In the mean time, as the moral influence of Germany alone must be amply sufficient to ensure the good government of the Duchies,

as far as that can be achieved by the almost
complete autonomy to which the Crown and
Legislature of the rest of the Danish dominions
have consented, the strife which has so long
subsisted might, it is evident, be effectually
closed by the adoption of that judicious proposal understood to have emanated from the
British Cabinet, by which the semi-sovereign
condition of the Duchies in their legislative
and administrative capacities should be secured
on the condition of their renunciation of their
"vote and interest" in the Germanic Confederation. By this they would be naturally
freed from their present liability to Prussian
influence ; and, one cause of perpetual misunderstanding removed, the pretensions of
Prussia to interfere in the domestic concerns
of her neighbour must be supported, if at all,
simply by open force. Of all the minor but
independent states in her vicinity, none has
more reason to look with distrust upon that

ambitious member of the sovereign brotherhood of European States than Denmark.

Some ardent theorists, of more comprehensive views than those which usually form the subject of speculation to practical men, and who love to look forward to a period when a redistribution of territory throughout Europe should be effected on principles very different in the main from those which have hitherto prevailed, have conceived, as a solution of the pending difficulties between Germany and Denmark, the adoption, as a boundary between the two populations, of the river Eider, the ancient limit of the empire of the Romans and of Charlemagne, and whereabouts the Teutonic language ceases to be spoken in unmixed purity; and the ultimate reunion of Denmark with the other Scandinavian crowns. By this arrangement the command of the Baltic would justly pertain to the race most interested in its preservation; and Germany and England, differing from, but not opposed to, each other or to Scandinavia, would constitute a powerful league mutually protecting and protected, yet never more than sufficiently so, against their common rivals. This league may be said to exist virtually, if it be not recognised; the principles of their social and political organization, their laws, the analogies of their language, the affinities of race prove it; their traditions and their aspirations secure it.

Every nation has undoubtedly been guilty, in the course of its career, of some fatal presumption or inconsistency of conduct, for which it has dearly paid; and of this truth there can be no more striking illustration than the punishment inflicted upon Denmark for its desertion of the cause of the Sea-Kings, in the attempt made by Gallic ambition to dispute the maritime supremacy of this country; the peculiar interest by which, in a material point of view, the Powers of the North are advantageously and naturally united. For a Scandinavian nation, whose most cherished traditions are "of the brine, briny," to combine with Sclave, or Gaul, or Teuton, against that free supremacy of the seas established and represented by the British flag, was a political solecism which providentially brought upon itself an early and enlightening chastisement. The peculiar lesson implied in those events alluded to — that, though Britain needs not their assistance, she looks for that practical respect from secondary maritime Powers which ensures at least their amicable eloignment from contests in which they are unable to act decisively — will probably not require to be repeated in that or any neighbouring quarter. That France or Germany should seek their alliance is only natural; and that they should accept an offer for mutual defence amongst themselves, and against the common object of their precautions, is just; for the superiority of one or other on land, and the value of the maritime forces at their command, in various possible complications, involving the designs of Russia or parts of Germany, is perfectly manifest: and since the integral territory of Norway and Sweden is now guaranteed by both France and England as against Russia, the most prudent course that Denmark could possibly adopt, for the security of her own entirety, would be the intimate and absolute alliance with France, however distasteful it might prove, for opposite reasons, both to Germany and Russia.

It is not often, it may be added, that in the views of superficial statesmen, or even those generally worthy of a better name, the political interests of France and England assume an aspect of patent and paramount identity; but in relation to one eventuality before adverted to, such may be said to be the case. To prevent Russia obtaining a footing in the Sound, by which means her navies might overawe the Northern Germanic countries, and intercept, threaten, or compete with the commerce of the world in that quarter, and especially of Great Britain and France, must ever be a matter of vital importance to the ruling authorities of those countries. In the face, therefore, of the insignificant resources of Denmark to resist a hostile attack from Russia, the treaty to which a few years ago each of those Powers was a party, wherein the claims of the Russian dynasty to the Holstein succession were formally recognised, may be looked upon, if not of questionable validity, as an ill-judged measure ; not the less objectionable because the adverse consequences apprehended from it may appear to be remote.

Of the internal constitution of these kingdoms but little need be said. In Denmark, independent of the Holstein question—which the Danes now threaten to settle with their own hand, and the expungement of which, whenever it occurs, will be a public blessing for which the human race ought to unite in voting some substantial testimonial of gratitude—its domestic policy, whether in the hands of a Rott-witz or a Madwig, is neither of a very hopeful nor exciting nature. It is just constitutional enough to ensure that mediocrity of progress which is generally safe, if never entirely satis-factory; and as to Royal authority, if the fact of every tenth man being a public official ap-pointed by the Crown, be any proof of what is meant by a strong government, Denmark might, indeed, afford a brilliant and encourag-ing example to all nations in search of that fugacious boon.

That Sweden and Norway—" a little more than kin, and less than kind "—are too nearly related to permit of actual union, would ap-pear, from the failure of all efforts in that direction, to afford a singular instance of

that wise disposition of nature which pre-
cludes the stagnation of society and its consequent degradation in these cold and conges-
tive regions of the world, where, if neighbouring people did not quarrel, they might, having
nothing else to do, possibly die of inaction.
Nature and Fortune have, therefore, it may be
supposed, provided a number of anomalies sufficient to keep alive that amount of discontent
necessary to vital movement in a people, however slow; inasmuch as, in addition to a reactionary legislature, presided over by a revolutionary dynasty, the peculiarity of the Swedish
constitution is that, while nominally liberal,
it is actually conservative to an unjust, and
therefore unsafe, degree. For, although it
embraces a system of representation, yet in
consequence of this being effected by means of
social classes strongly, or rather violently, demarked from each other, a proper fusion is
thereby prohibited of the political elements of

national life; and the true result of constitutional government being wanting, the weight of legislative power tends towards the greater numerical force embodied in the stationary sections of the clergy and the landed proprietary.

RUSSIA.

RUSSIA.

———◇———

RUSSIA, the representative of the Scythia and Sarmatia of antiquity, the type of irresponsible power, the symbol and significator of material despotism, is naturally distinguished by a policy selfish and saturnine, and in its application all but monotonously successful.

It has been a matter of wonder to some that for so long a time the schism between the Greek Catholic and Roman Catholic Churches has been permitted to endure ; and until the commencement of the eighteenth century reasonable hopes were entertained on the part of pious doctors of the Western communion that offensive differences might be eliminated, and a

salutary union between the spiritual rivals
effected.   But after the adoption of the headship of the Russo-Greek Church into his secular
sovereignty by Peter the Great, those hopes
vanished.   It is now the object and interest of
Russia to maintain and widen the schism, for
as, in matters of faith, a spiritual sovereignty if
at issue with a secular one would necessarily to a
piously disposed mind appear invested with superior sanction,—the opposing authority, though
never so haughty and potent in its civil aspect,
would beyond doubt proportionately suffer in
point of prestige.   All chance of this state of
things being now nullified by the union of the
spiritual and secular authority in the Imperial
Crown, the infallibility of a Pope is at once
protected and practically enforced by the omni-
potence of the Emperor.

As solemnity adds dignity to every act of
State, and dignity is an essential attribute of
power, it has been the invariable custom of

Russia—in all her diplomatic dealings with the states of the Continent, as well as by her own official and, as occasion serves, non-recognized interference with European populations, those especially of Sclavonic or Roumaic race—to sanctify all political projects, whatever their motive or purport, by an appeal to the superior independence of the Greek Catholic Church; in which, apart from the authority of the Emperor, no power exists capable of modifying to the extent of a hair's breadth the bases of faith as already and of old established; and at the same time of putting forward the Imperial Government as the invincible champion of the freedom and purity of orthodox Christianity.

That in these pretensions is a certain amount of sincerity—for in proportion as men are ignorant they are undoubtedly sincere—and in their maintenance a certain degree of good, must be conceded; the latter, because it may be taken as an axiom that the predominance of priestly power is more prejudicial to human progress, whether considered socially or intellectually, than any political despotism the world has known; and that there are limits in subserviency beyond which the most arbitrary governments do not wish to trespass; and the former, because they have been systematically asserted under the test of powerful hostility and severe humiliation.

But as regards those countries among whose populations the championship of a particular form of Christianity would constitute no claim to admiration or veneration, but rather the reverse, Russia very cautiously abstains from obtruding upon Turk, Tahtar, or Chinese, the fanatical aspect of her adamantine character; and, quite content with subduing, never dreams of converting enemies, who by adoption of Western creeds and habits of thought, might speedily become inoculated with notions of Western liberty, and finally perhaps prove more dangerous as subjects than as foes.

And this is a consistent and intelligible policy; dictated first by a sense of the necessity of self-preservation, and ultimately adapted by a not unnatural expansion of principles to the furtherance of those schemes of aggression, which, resulting in the grandeur and predominance of a particular people, certainly but indirectly contribute to national good, the enhancement of its positive value and repute among the nations of the world.

The primary policy of Russia has therefore a religious front; and this it is which gives generally so much of dignity and weight to her influence in Europe; and partly because her religion is not of a missionary, argumentative, or combative character, in which there is frequently much of implied disadvantage, but avoiding controversy is simply affirmative, in the face of all varieties of the Christian faith, of its own absolute truth and pre-eminent orthodoxy.

And although it is at all times difficult to disentangle the political from those religious considerations by which her public conduct appears to be overtly or ostensibly at least determined, this becomes in the Eastern or Turkish question, both from the immense importance of the matter and the mystery in which it is involved, an almost utter impossibility. Constantinople itself, the queenly city which appears to dominate two continents, is not more attractive to the Imperial government from its commanding position, abundant resources, and luxurious environs, than to the humblest peasant of the salt and sterile steppe, from its being the sacred birthplace of the faith which he professes. Whatever, therefore, the motives by which the Government of the State may be actuated in its relations to Turkey directly, or its oblique relations with other Powers in reference to the Sultan's dominions, the religious element of Russian policy constitutes a basis which the most illiterate or obtuse intellect may appreciate; and illustrates that perfect identity of State and people, awful almost in its extent and simplicity, which subsists and operates habitually within the bounds—if such a term be applicable—of that mighty empire. In that empire the unit is as the whole; there is neither majority nor minority; all movement is uniformal; religion, race, and government, form as it were with their intersecting influences one circular system of centralized authority.

Let the ultimate fate of Turkey be what it may, the policy of Russia in respect to the East must be held to have culminated in those measures which led to the Crimean war; but as it culminated it exploded. Upon the considerations connected with this fatally grand event, which has undoubtedly shaken and somewhat loosened in certain directions the system of

Europe, it would be inexpedient on the present occasion to dilate. It began as all remember with an ecclesiastical wrangle about the possession of the keys of the Holy Sepulchre. When these melancholy words were first whispered round among statesmen and diplomatists, there were but few even of those who assisted or presided in the chancelleries of their respective states to whom that ominous expression suggested that the key to another chamber of death which was about to number its inmates by thousands of thousands, situated beside the then secluded city of an inland sea, was soon to be unlocked by that ensanguined key, the sword, which has already opened to mankind the entrance of so many miseries. What began with a squabble between a handful of Greek and Latin monks, speedily developed itself as a contest between the three chief empires of the world. The ultimate object of the Russian Autocrat was no secret ; and that object

France and Great Britain were naturally and by every motive of sound policy bound to defeat.

So long as Russia remains the great homogeneous power she is, unequalled in quantity, unbroken in continuity, with an overpowering predominance in two continents, and considerable territorial extension in a third,—held together as this dominion is, not by those slack and easily severable ties by which the colonial possessions of this country are attached to the British Crown, but in a strict and stern union, —it is only right and reasonable that the other leading Powers of Europe should do their utmost to preclude if possible all further aggrandisement on her part in any quarter: much more, therefore, in her obtaining possession of a city which is itself the crown of the world, and which in her hands would give her the command of the Mediterranean, and in fact universal supremacy.

If one can only imagine her designs in Poland, Hungary, Servia, Bosnia, and elsewhere, eventually realised, and herself firmly seated in the midst of faithful populations, with Constantinople for her southern and Petersburg her northern capital—her fleets sweeping the Baltic and the Mediterranean and the Northern Seas; and her armies, by their number alone less formidable than by their servile devotion, along with that of the multitudinous people from whom they spring, to the irresponsible will of one man, over-lording the Sclavonic continent,—it needs but little argument to justify in the minds of Western statesmen, of Keltic or Teutonic stock, any political combinations which may avail against the possibility of such calamities.

Without indulging, as certain writers do, in the habit of holding up Russia on all occasions and in all junctures as a gigantic hobgoblin to the rest of Europe, it is not unwise to contemplate contingencies; and it can do us no harm to bear in mind that a race which looks upon its chief as a god, and whose only social instincts, so far as manageable in masses, are war and religion, is a dangerous race to those addicted to the practice of the arts of peace, the study of philosophy and science, free speculation and inquiry, and belief in the beneficial efficacy of public opinion resulting from the unrestricted and amicable communion of a vast variety of classes ; and that while the unlimited progress of other European races is far from being fraught with danger to the liberties or the enlightened civilisation of other nations, that of Sclavonism as at present constituted is tantamount to the cultivation of an unitarian despotism hostile to human happiness. This despotism nevertheless the Sclavonic family are found fondly to favour, because although it somewhat reduces them as a people in point of political privileges, which they little regard, it exalts them as a race.

But although Russian policy, as already stated, attained in the Mentschikoff negotiations its point of greatest elongation, and failed, yet, without dwelling any longer upon that event, it must be allowed that the same course, though in a less haughty attitude, is still pursued; and appears calculated, unless met with perpetual opposition equally vigilant and strenuous, to be ultimately attended with permanent, as it is even now with temporary, success. In this success is the evidence of a striking peculiarity of Russian policy in relation especially to all the semi-civilised communities of the East. Other nations exert an influence undoubtedly more or less natural or justifiable, as the case may be, or as circumstances may require; but Russian influence can only be described as pressure—on all sides incessantly accumulating pressure.

If to these considerations, which justly arise in the mind from contemplating the situation

and social condition, the commercial interests
and prospects, the capabilities and expectations
natural and political, of these rich, important,
and yet imperfectly developed regions, such
as the Principalities, Bosnia, Servia, Roumelia, and others which nominally pertain
to Turkey, partially acknowledge her suze-
rainty or rejoice in the assertion of an independence they are incapable of exercising, but
the populations of which, from other motives,
to which allusion has already been made, en-
tertain more regard and openly affect more
submission towards Russia herself—we add the
spell of her immense power, her active protectorate of the common faith, her organized
and recognized pecuniary retainership among
the subjects of other states, we may not be
surprised at the effect which the control of
this powerful machinery, moral and physical
is calculated and intended to produce,—namely,
the disintegration of the Turkish Empire. We

shall be compelled only to admit that nothing
but the united efforts of the other great Powers,
Great Britain and France combined, with some
renewed vigour and vitality in its own internal
system, can suffice to sustain it for even a
moderate period. Should this resisting power
be diminished or attenuated in any sensible
degree by a misunderstanding between France
and Great Britain, its downfall is certain. The
solution of the Eastern question, indeed, simply
signifies the dissolution of the Turkish Empire,
primarily; and, secondly, the substitution of
another " Power " in its place. If left to itself
there is every reason to believe Turkey would
soon die a natural death; and the doubt hu-
manely arises in the mind of a spectator whether
a natural death be not preferable to an unnatural life. But supposing this to be so in
ordinary cases, in this one many most potent and
absorbing considerations, because inwoven with
the strongest passions of humanity, the hopes

and fears of nations, induce, strangely enough, those most interested in the decease of the sufferer to struggle to prolong his life.

There is no other European nation at present constituted, and of first rank, which would or could dream of occupying as its capital the city of the Sultan. But Russia has set her heart upon it. On the other hand, except under the pressure of defeat which it seems impossible seriously to contemplate, to afford her that gratification would be little short of absolute insanity on the part of the nations of the West. It would be the abdication of a superior power in behalf of an inferior—inferior in all respects except that massive yet pointed unity of organisation, civil and military, proper to their race, and which has enabled them to act with such tremendous force hitherto in the affairs of the world.

Russia, it is said by some, on the contrary, is an advancing, improving Power. She only lacks a more commanding sea-board, a more genial clime, a more direct intercourse with the civilising tendencies of the South—the sunny cestus of the globe, to secure the love and admiration of the human race, and to take her proper place at the head of universal progress, as the leader of religious order in the State, and the patroness of conservative piety in the Church; and that the substitution of her dominion, or indeed of any other Christian Power, for the effete and barbarous sway of the Seraglio, (for that should be the diplomatic title of the Turkish Government rather than the Porte) with its thousands of unhappy victims, masculine and female, its unconscionable corruption and political profligacy, and its legalised system of extortion towards its own subjects, the majority of whom are of course Christians—would be a blessing to the world. And much of this, so far as the assertion of the more general proposition extends, is indubitable; but that Russia is that Power which the world wishes to see, or would be benefited by seeing, substituted for Turkey, is, indeed, more than doubtful. There are peculiarities observable in her character and constitution which forbid the voluntary entertainment by others for a single moment of such a project. Upon this Great Britain, France, and Austria are in sworn trine, or in absolute conjunction.

Before dismissing this question, it is of course to be conceded that the perpetuation of the Ottoman power, if not by its own inherent vigour, at least by the antagonistic inclinations of others, and the opposing forces brought to bear at different angles by the various converging interests of surrounding nations, may yet by bare possibility be secured in its own despite ; and in this respect, and this only, its maintenance may be considered as contributing, under the universal impartiality of Divine decrees, to a more humane and liberal government of mankind than might take place, were such a position not fortunately occupied by an Eastern people, of Mohammedan profession and a fierce and fanatical disposition; their presence on the verge of a continent professing a religion practically patronising persecution and aggression on all other forms of faith, constituting a pledge for good behaviour, equally valid, it is obvious, in opposite directions, and operative even to the very extremities of the globe.

To affirm, as the partizans of Russia and some writers among ourselves have done, that the Turks have no right to be in Europe, because they are Mohammedans, is virtually to assert one of two things: either that Christians only have a right to live where they please, and enjoy the fruits of their conquests; or to admit that we have no right in Asia or elsewhere than in our own immediate quarter of the world. To fall back upon the superiority of religion, race, enlightenment, art, science, or what not, is as unsatisfactory a process in disputing with Turks as kicking against thorns; for these are the very points in debate, and involve the possible expansion of the principle and its application among ourselves to a fatal and even internecine degree.

Still it is undoubtedly to be wished for the sake of the Christian population of those fine and fertile provinces constituting European Turkey, and who manifestly cannot sympathize intimately with the government, both severe and careless, under which they find themselves, that some solution of their political difficulties satisfactory to themselves, to Europe, and to that formidable Power whose protection is so oppressive, should yet be attained. If, therefore, at any time it should happen (and in certain circumstances it may be permissible to suppose a case—say, at the death of a Sultan) that the confusion of affairs social, political, and perhaps financial, were such as to induce, in the face of divided councils or rival claimants to the succession, the Christian population of the metropolis and the surrounding districts, gradually perhaps embracing the whole of European Turkey, to rise in self-vindication of their natural independence, and, without bloodshed or unjustifiable outrage, render themselves lords of the crisis; and suppose this state of things effected by the joint efforts, where practicable, of both denominations of Christians; and measures taken judiciously and not improbably in concert with the ministers of Foreign Powers, for the permanent establishment, with popular consent, of a monarchical government, regularly organized, not too theoretical in its construction, nor impracticably liberal in the popular element of its constitution, guaranteed, it may be, ultimately by the collective protectorate as at present existing,—such an event, there is no doubt, would form the best and the only natural solution of the Eastern question. It would remove from Christendom the irritating anomaly of Moslem domination and the peril of a mighty and desolating contest always impending; it would introduce a sense of tranquillity, security, and dignity among the inhabitants, which has never been experienced by them during nearly half a millennium. In a material point of view it would lead to an immense expansion of the natural resources of that district, and which it principally requires now to render it one of the most prosperous in the world; while as a State, from its variety of genealogical sub-divisions, it would operate as a check to Russia politically; and as a rival, ecclesiastically, with doubtless the best effect upon the religious sympathies of the entire Greek Catholic persuasion, which is now left universally exposed to the designs of Russia throughout the world, simply from the fact that she forms the only Power professing the same faith which occupies a dominant position among the nations of the earth.

Whether such a movement as that just sketched by way of hypothesis were likely to extend itself to the neighbouring kingdom of Greece, and with what effect, it will of course be impossible to speak with certainty; but there is reason to suspect, from the late Czar's contemptuous expressions of opposition to any idea of the aggrandisement of that state, that such a result would be neither improbable nor unwelcome to the most considerable portion of the intelligent and wealthy classes of Roumelia, Macedonia, Southern Thrace, and other important regions. To all these populations the disadvantages of a state so small and comparatively unproductive as Greece are already sufficiently obvious; while, on the other hand, as the basis of an organisation actually established, a settled government, a constitutional sovereignty, an army, a navy, an independent commercial class, enjoying recognition in all the richest and most important countries of Europe, and practising negotiations with success in all departments of trade, present the prospect of too many and considerable benefits derivable from such an amalgamation to be altogether discarded as impracticable or impolitic by disinterested well-wishers of a rising people, in deference to the selfish prejudices of a haughty and overreaching competitor.

Such being the perils, attractions, and capabilities of the Oriental question in the abstract, to Russia, many of which remain in full force, it may not be uninstructive, nor perhaps unadvisable, if we are to estimate rightly the grandeur of the arc of Russian policy, to retrace, briefly and rapidly as can be, the actual development of these conditions, in the position, and bearings upon each other, of the European Powers generally interested in this greatest of political problems.

The original complications of France, Russia, and the Porte, as regards the matter of the shrines, the lighting of lamps, and the locking of doors, which ostensibly gave occasion to the subsequent unreasonable demands of the Russian Emperor, having been disposed of by voluntary retractation on the part of the French Government, the reproach of originating the late calamitous war is justly laid at the door of the Russian people, of whose territorial cupidity and fanatical ambition Nicholas was, both by position and sympathy, the exponent and the head. His foregone conclusions upon this point are clearly proved by his dramatic conversations with Sir H. Seymour, and sufficiently known by what may be signified as his "deep-sea soundings" at a prior period. Distrusting any possible degree of integrity in the Turkish Government, and discouraging, from motives which it is needless to characterise, the slightest tendency to improvement, either of an administrative or popular character, in the affairs of the State, and less accurately than ambitiously informed, it is to be feared, by his agents, of its political and commercial position, both advancing, the Emperor—who evidently considered it entirely from an enthusiastic point of view—believed that the last hour of "the sick man" had chimed; and he was anxious to take advantage of the inevitable dissolution, as he conceived, of that State, before any revolutionary projects could be brought to weigh, at such a juncture, upon the necessarily agitated condition of Europe, and to forestall the interference of any other Power at that probable crisis.

But, as the world cannot be turned upside down in a corner, and as the destruction of a very considerable state must be attended with circumstances of some publicity, and as every sacrifice requires salt, his Imperial Majesty found it necessary to prepare in a certain degree the minds of other governments for the great events which he intended to produce, but which he wished to be considered self-evolving.

Proposals similar to those he had made personally at our own Court in 1844, he had caused to be made or insinuated, between that period and 1852, to the French Cabinet; but not finding them responded to in the manner he had anticipated, the Emperor appears to have thought less and less of the once wished-for concurrence of France, from that incapable and degraded state, the natural effect of unrestrained democracy, into which it was supposed to have been precipitated by the revolutionary outbreak of 1848, and the unsupported and despicable machinations of the preceding system of government. Believing, moreover, from the condition of affairs in Austria, and the civil and pecuniary embarrassments of that state, which, by owing its national preservation to his friendly suppression of the Hungarian rebellion, had become, by the consequent gratitude of its people—the ruling classes, at least—and the youth and inexperience of its ruler, almost a dependency of Russia, or so far that he might with tolerable certainty calculate upon its non-interference with any schemes of his own; and that, in fact, as His Imperial Majesty failed not to remark, "What would suit him, would suit Austria;" while Prussia, as if in anticipation of the minute and ignominious part to be taken by her throughout, he never once named, her interests as a then satellite of Russia seeming altogether out of the lists,—it appeared clear to the mind of the Emperor that, by the connivance and with the complicity of England, to whom "the flesh-pots of Egypt" and Candia might serve as allurements, opposition from any other quarter would be perfectly nugatory. Of Greece, although so inconsiderable a state as regards area, and generally an "accessory after the fact" to his own policy, whatever it might be, Nicholas seems to have entertained some jealousy—a jealousy not occasioned by any manifestations on the part of the Greek Cabinet—to him subservient enough, German enough, and only quasi-national in spirit itself—but by views which might possibly be advanced on behalf of the Queen of the South, in case of the disruption of the Ottoman Seignory, by the Western and more liberal Powers of the Continent, who had formerly stood sponsors for the nascent nation of the Ægean—concerning which his suspicions might colourably arise from the relative traditions possessed in common by Greece and Russia and Byzantium with reference to the orthodox faith and the political domination of the East. Any event of this description, as was before intimated, tending to a counterbalance of Russian influence and protection in the affairs of the Greek Catholic faith, he naturally deprecated and most earnestly desired to avoid. Emphatically, therefore, did the Emperor denounce, in any contingency whatever connected with the expected break-up of the Osmanli dominions, permission of the slightest political advantage or territorial aggrandisement to Greece.

The juncture seemed favourable; and, if his information had been correct, the Emperor's reasoning, from the point of view universally adopted by his people, was substantially justifiable; for there can be no question that in such an eventuality as that contemplated, the positive interests of Russia subtend a palpably greater area than the negative and always partially divergent interests of Great Britain and France. But these, if neither equal separately to the first, nor perfectly equivalent between each other, on all grounds, are still sufficient to prevent the un-

K

natural preponderance too likely to accrue from the realisation of such a project as that alluded to; and this the Emperor discovered too late—having omitted to compute the elements of one other, and one only, possible combination by which that defeat could be effected.

An union of sentiment between the cabinets of a newly-elected republican autocrat and the rigidly constitutional sovereign of Great Britain appeared, without doubt, to the Imperial cogitations the most preposterous of suppositions; particularly while individuals of the latter Government were publicly denouncing the conduct and character of the new French potentate, the somewhat hearty acceptance of whose advent to power by another distinguished member had occasioned a serious internal division in the Ministry; and while, throughout the land, the British Press, with unrivalled generosity and foresight, were alternating between the not very consistent prophecies of French invasion and French downfall—between joy over the statistics of a decreasing population, and dread of an increasing power.

Relying, therefore, on the sincerity of this display of cordial misunderstanding, and the hereditary hostility of the two nations, Nicholas ordered demands to be made of Turkey in relation to the protectorate of the Greek Christians which were palpably inconsistent with the Sultan's rights of sovereignty in his own dominions. To the audacious matter of these demands, Prince Menschikoff, the Imperial Envoy, added that insolence to the Porte and that general arrogance of manner which fortunately aroused, to an unwonted degree, the indignant attention of all the resident diplomats of Constantinople : who hesitated not to express both publicly and privately their marked disapproval of such uncourteous demeanour to a friendly Power ; and which has stamped the delivery of this message with a peculiar and ineffaceable infamy.

These demands, by the judicious and spirited advice of the representatives of France and England at the court of the Sultan, were resisted. Modifications proposed on the part of the latter were refused. An ultimatum, additionally offensive on the side of Russia, was rejected; and the Prince retired.

Notwithstanding the somewhat ominous conjuncture in opinion and advice of the representatives of these two courts at Constantinople, Nicholas, on the departure of his Envoy Extraordinary, finding that his projects had been reciprocally communicated to each other by the Western Powers, and unitedly condemned, abandoned all further disguise of his intentions, and ordered the occupation of the Danubian Principalities. The Pruth was accordingly passed, and Jassy and other places occupied by Russian troops, by command of the Emperor, as a material guarantee in the event of the Porte finally refusing submission to his terms.

It was at this crisis that the design of Turkey as a dissolving view settled, unfortunately, into a steady transparency, about which there could be no misconception. But as the detail of events is not here to be looked for, and as from this point the flowers of diplomacy were rapidly transfigured into fruits of war—of which most now living have enjoyed at least a mouthful, in the shape of income-tax and other necessaries of life—it will be sufficient to add that it was the unlooked-for and almost incredible union of the governments, legislatures, peoples, and armies, for the time being, of France and England in a policy at once just, generous, and sagacious, that has given new life and increased certainty to the principle of national independence; and the vindication of the fact that, in the dealings of governments, as of man with man, right is to be considered before race or religion. How far beyond the radius of this truth—and men often pay dearest for the simplest lessons—the world at large or the more immediate belligerents profited by the war, will probably never be precisely communicated to each other. One thing is obvious, that the introduction of Sardinia into the contest, like the addition of a fraction to the sum of millions, sensibly diminished at the time—though, not being thought of now, it has ceased to impair— the general impressiveness of the event; for that England and France united should require the assistance of the arms of a petty state which it was necessary to subsidise, and not more immediately concerned in the conflict than Switzerland or Belgium, it were unreasonable to suppose. The three vast and ultimate elements of European society, neither of which can be vanquished or even seriously invalidated except by union of the two others, were in deadly shock; and such an interference was as uncalled-for as ineffectual. Another remark to be made by way of conclusion is, that, whether for the better or the worse, the circumstances of her defeat have led naturally to a somewhat sullen isolation of Russia from the other governments of Europe, and a professed indifference towards them, the effect of which on the great Conservative party of the Continent, whose ostensible leadership was vested in the Imperial Czar, may be traced, to the joy of some and the discontent of others, in that position of manifest disparagement which the legitimist and dynastic interests of various nations now occupy. Aggression in the East and conservatism in the West formed the plot and underplot of the drama in which Russia was before that period engaged; but another stage and another character may lie before her.

In relation to Poland enough has been already said to render it unnecessary to spend much

time in moralising over the changes of sub-
lunary affairs. Poland was a Power in Europe
when the Dukes of Muscovy exercised about as
much influence on the events of the world as
do at present the Princes of Monaco; and when
the head of the Teutonic knights, predecessors
of his Prussian Majesty, received with humble
thankfulness the gift of part only of the province
from which the present royal title is derived.

The Poles were always a turbulent and un-
steady people, and—too much addicted, from
the earliest periods of their history even to the
present time, to "sublime and sanguinary
manifestations," to use the lofty language of
their most recent protest—themselves provoked
finally the fate to which they succumbed; and
remain a lasting monument to the civilised
world of the consequences of a people, surrounded by governments possessing a regularly
organised delegation of social authority, claiming for themselves the privileges of a barbarous

liberty wholly incompatible with the interests of advanced society.

The Poles, for the most part Roman Catholics, neglecting all practicable improvements, and still devoted to the pursuit of their one grand impossibility, may be distinguished as of all the nations of Europe the most highly uneducated. In the mean time, the toleration even of their religion as Roman Catholic is another of those points which the subtilty and craft of the Russian Government has established as a means of control ; for so long as the Poles retain any recollection of their independency, and so long as the necessity of securing possession of the land—a yard westward being well worth a mile eastward—is imperative in the mind of the governing race and dynasty, so long the policy of precluding the possibility of complete sympathy among the people, and of keeping open, in fact, a source of disaccord, which can always be intensified into animosity as occasion may serve between any two classes, or races united in nothing but subjection to the same Imperial Crown, and not unwilling to be the instruments of each other's degradation, is too obvious to require further proof, or those parallels even which might be adduced from other governments more popularly responsible.

Neither are the Poles entirely exempt from liability to reproach in their dealings with others; their treatment of the Cossacks for two hundred years has rendered those tribes their hereditary foes; and the presence of these at Warsaw, Lublin, Mödlin, and other carefully watched places in that kingdom, is in unison with the general tenor of history and all state policy in such matters; based as it is upon a principle which Great Britain also has acknowledged, and upon which she still acts.

Since the accession of the present Emperor, the intentions of the Russian Government towards Poland, as evinced by acts, have been both liberal and amicable; so much so that further concessions are impossible, without danger at least of exciting the jealousy of other portions of the empire. For not only Poland but Finland and Lithuania have recollections of constitutions, the separate existence and rival action of which would doubtless be inimical to that imperial unity of administration which it has been the perpetual aim of Russia to establish throughout her dominions.

The Sclavonian mind, it may be assumed, as a general rule, is rather imitative and appreciative than logical or speculative; and while devoted to unity of sentiment and demonstrations in mass, seems not to be endowed with that energy which in Kelt and Teuton in their combinations is ever prompting the individual to eminence in arts, or civil life, or even to martyrdom in these pursuits, nor for the attainment and transmission of popular liberties.

Great exertions are lavished with theatrical pomp on puerile demonstrations, which might be reserved for more effective purposes. A peculiar costume, a fanciful arrangement of colours, a torrent of sentiment, strikes an observer from its uniformity as fictitious, or mechanical; the object being multiplied, the effect of the impression is proportionately diminished. A family in mourning excites our sympathies; but a nation in mourning has the effect which a ceremony or spectacle intended to be impressive might be expected to have. This is not the way in which liberty has been won by those who loved it best, and best knew how to obtain that highest of earthly blessings. But although the Poles have at all times made but ill use of their opportunities, vainly enacting impossibilities, and giving authority to suicidal absurdities,—demanding absolute unanimity in a deliberative multitude, and dignifying with a kingly veto every individual member of an ill-assorted, irresponsible, and eminently corrupt assembly, — yet it cannot be concealed that Poland has a certain claim to sympathy which Europe recognizes; and that while the troubles of Russia in Poland are likely enough to synchronize with the abolition of serfage, the position of that province adjoining now constitutionally-governed countries, independently of its history, necessitates probably at no very distant period—whatever internal complications in other quarters of the Russian empire may be the result—political concessions of a substantial and satisfactory nature. These concessions, if sought with prudence and pacific perseverance, may unquestionably be looked for with confidence; but the misfortune is that a party, as headstrong as it is weak-brained, is counselling measures of a totally different tendency, and which involves the assertion of national independence—a ghost which refuses to be laid, but still only a ghost.

In the mean time it is owing to the reciprocal relations of Hungary and Poland to Russia and Austria, which are to each other in the position of contradictories and sub-contraries, their mutual interests directly amicable and obliquely hostile, that the gloomy discord of the two empires has not before now broken out into more fatally overt manifestations.

Siberia, in respect to that nucleus of empire which has been located in various times at Novgorod, Moscow, and Petersburg, and which appears to have at present a strong tendency to gravitate towards the shores of the Bosphorus, being almost entirely unproductive to its Imperial owner of moral or political influence, exhibits but the splendid powerlessness of a cometary appendage. The voice of its people is never heard; Europe only knows of it as a land of snows, and fogs, and furs, of mines and pines. To a Russian criminal, however, whether real or supposed, the name Siberia signifies that

comparative degree of punishment to which
death ranks only as positive ; supplying, indeed,
an equivalent to purgatory among the professors of a creed deficient in that potential
article of belief, so reasonable, so consolatory,
and withal so remunerative.

Yet it must be admitted that in the relations
of Russia with China, more intimate and
favoured than those of any other people, an
indirect aspect of rivalry, commercial and
political, brings intermittently this enormous
province within the scope of British observa-
tion ; while its territorial position with regard
to Persia, Tartary, and the many minor inde-
pendencies of Central Asia, restless and refluent
as the sands of their deserts, excites perpetually
an instinctive caution in the minds of the
Trade-kings of the East, the Lords of India,
who forget not that it was to Russian intrigues
we owe the Affghan war; and that as the
progress of Russia is inevitably towards more

fertile districts and positions more potential than those she at present occupies, her object is undoubtedly to obtain a commanding point upon the Eastern Ocean both for naval and commercial purposes. Whoever else may sleep, Russia is watchful over expiring empires; and is always ready to administer such death-bed consolations as the successor to power has naturally on his tongue. Her advance in this direction has been uniformly stealthy but steady. But it is possible that too much success may some time shake the solidity of her empire. And at all events, in case of "anything happening" to the Chinese empire, it may become a question which only an Imperial Legislature can solve, whether our own petty possessions at Hong-Kong would be found sufficient as a fulcrum for the support of British interests in that important region.

But although Russia has doubtless her mission, external and internal, to fulfil, among the national families of the world; and although she has, partly during the great Revolutionary war, given evidence of what that mission is, as well as by her conduct and attitude since the Congress of Vienna, both with regard to the events of the last forty-five years and the observance of treaties—a conduct and attitude eminently distinguished by a consistency and dignity appropriate to the great conservative power of the Continent; yet, since the Crimean war, which, if it effected nothing else, had the glory of having broken up for ever the offensive confederacy of the double-headed eagles, it cannot fail to have been observed that Russia, whether from motives of choice or necessity, has shown but a very inactive and reluctant interest in the affairs of Western Europe. And for her own sake, and in face of her own internal difficulties, this is probably the wisest and safest course she could pursue. The time is gone by, it may be hoped, when

Russia appeared, and with some reason, in the imagination of many, to occupy towards the rest of Europe a position analogous to that of Macedon towards the states of Greece in the days of Demosthenes,—and the suggestion is uneasy enough; but to such the reflection must be consoling, that just as her last foes, the brave mountaineers of Caucasus, have been vanquished, and the first symptoms of territorial repletion manifested by this constrictor of nations, her attention should now be, as it probably for a long time will be, mainly, if not exclusively, centred in herself.

By the measures recently adopted by the Imperial Government in relation to the serfs, the general population being elevated, the relative position of immense classes and strata of society is, of course, dislocated—to be found perhaps, at some future time, ranged against each other in anticlinal attitude. In any case the initial struggles of a nation towards freedom are always attended with painful or disastrous circumstances; and since her troubles appear seriously to have commenced, and it is difficult and even distressing to contemplate the possibility of an irresponsible despotism exercised over fifty or sixty millions of free men, the present system of government will have infallibly to give way; in which event the achievement of national benefit depends naturally on the character the contest may assume.

Democracy is the most—perhaps it might be said the only—artificial form of government, and if man were entirely a pure intelligence it might even be characterized as the most reasonable. But having a blended constitution in which instincts and passions frequently opposed to the dictates and deductions of reason play the most important part, mankind in general have found it safer and on the whole more conducive to their happiness to be content with a less pretentious position than that which by the strict division of human rights they would be justified in assuming. If men were not secretly conscious of this fact, what despotic force could withstand the merely expressed wish of a united people; a power which like the mesmerist has only to say "I will, so and so," and dynasties and despotisms vanish? But the truth is that men, instinctively knowing themselves better than political theorists can teach them, have always sought safety in a power able to repress and control themselves, giving sufficient effect to the demand of a general sense of justice that it should act on all sides with uniform pressure. This security different nations have found according to the innate characteristics of race, religion, culture, and other disposing circumstances, in various forms of government. The pure and simple races find it in despotism; which is not tyranny, but in certain conditions of society an express result of the popular will. The mixed races,

more advanced in civilization and general
social condition, look for this security rather
under classified institutions and complex political systems, endowed with self-reparative and
expansive energies.

Russia, it need scarcely be said, will be long
before she arrives at such a condition; but, unhappily, it sometimes happens that in periods
of political agitation, visionaries and enthusiasts
will precipitate conclusions for which the more
cautious section of society, being wholly un-
prepared, are fain to relapse into extremes
which cause the fruitless ruin of an originally
well-intended enterprise. Revolutionary tendencies, it may be taken for granted in Russia,
may be and would be defeated; endeavours for
a share in the government, as a right, by
certain sections of the nobility and people
are far more easy to be conceived, and would
be far more difficult to subdue.

But if the Emperor be not prepared to concede

something in this way, he had better not have
released the serfs from servitude; for their discontent will probably become greater than
before, and if greater, more embarrassing; as
they will have naturally become possessed of
an order of ideas and opinions which find no
legitimate means of development and expression.

Should this ever prove the tendency of things
in Russia, and representative institutions at any
time be established, there would require to be
provided, for the proper working of the system,
different centres and limitations of localities;
and this, it is possible, may supply the means
by which the divulsion of the empire may be
effected, undesignedly perhaps, but doubtless
beneficially. For it seems unreasonable to
suppose that this mighty aggregate of nations
and territories should always, or even for long,
enjoy that perilous pre-eminence which would
necessarily pertain to it as an integral power;

and which as one and indivisible, though of an inferior character morally and politically, it at present occupies.

Lastly, this may be noted, that however available it may have been in times past for aggressive purposes, the social constitution of Russia, though superficially regular, and somewhat elaborately organized, is, in view especially of the new order of things inaugurated by the recent reforms, essentially defective. The nobility, though hereditary, have no real power as a class in the government of the State, and no substantial privileges of a public character but those attached to them as individual officeholders, in a manner and for a period entirely at the discretion of the crown. Neither have the citizen class any political rights or immunities, except also as individuals invested with official authority. All power devolves downwards upon the people; nothing emanates from them. The only aspect in which Russian society is capable of being viewed with any degree of satisfaction, is in its intimate connexion with the land, in which all classes, even those of the lowest degree of serfdom, are inalienably interested. Russia, therefore, which has already announced herself as one of the powers of the future, and is evidently looking forward to a vast extension of her influence at no distant date in the affairs of the world, presents the somewhat singular spectacle of an autocracy based upon practical socialism. Hitherto, by permission of superior authority, and to a limited extent in certain literary circles in one or other of her capitals, opinions have not been altogether without their representative organs; but the contemplation of a vast and entire nation without any rights of their own, and not ever likely, therefore, to pay much respect to the rights of others, claiming proudly for their chief ally the great democratic Power of the New World, is not suggestive of very confiding or encouraging reflections to the supporters of constitutional governments, and the originators and conservators of civil and religious freedom, equally against the tyranny of the one or the multitude.

To what extent the new Imperial scheme of emancipation will operate, and how far the interests of the class proposed to be benefited, formerly restricted to the land, may become modified by their freedom, has yet to be seen. Their gain in one direction may possibly be counterbalanced by their loss in another. At the same time the stereotyped immobility of Russian society as an universal characteristic is lost. A fluctuating class will be at the disposal of the Government, which may possibly enable it to fortify itself against popular movements not unlikely to ensue, and the issue of which may eventually prove of the highest consequence to other and distant nations, as well as to " all the Russias."

FRANCE.

FRANCE.

I⊤ is not uninteresting to observe, that all the great states of the West are, ethnologically, to borrow a term from a sister science, of conglomerate formation. In some the constituent elements are combined in more equal proportions than in others: the former being the case in Great Britain, which may be considered Kelto-Teutonic; and Austria and Prussia, as each a mixture, though in different ratios, of German and Sclavonic population. On the other hand, the two most homogeneous empires of Europe are Russia and France. In France, at the commencement of the historical epoch, the Gauls—akin to the Gäel of Caledonia, the

Galatians of Asia Minor, the Kelts, and the
Kymri of Wales, or Galles—are found undis-
puted possessors of the land. No traces, at
least, of an earlier people in that capacity—out
of the Drift—are discoverable. With these
the Romans—their conquerors, and themselves
of a kindred race—largely intermixed ; and
finally, the Franks—a clan of Belgic Gauls, of
mixed origin, and producing but little effect,
apart from their conquest, on the general population—after subduing a small section of the
country, finally succeeded in imposing their
name upon the whole. Upon antecedents like
these depend the nature and direction of national
policy. Pure races are always of an aggressive
character, nor is it until they become mixed
that they become stationary or contented. Different varieties even of the same stock perpetually contend together, until a social combination has been satisfactorily effected. These
characteristics, however, of race—wherever the

battle-ground was situated, whether in Germany, Belgium, or Italy—may be considered as originating in the natural rivalry of Kelt and Teuton. While it is difficult to say which has gained or suffered more than the other, the result, as at present shown by territorial possessions, is satisfactory enough, both in its present aspects and future probabilities. The aggressive, or rather dictatorial, character of French policy is doubtless owing, in a great degree, to the comparative unity of origin of the mass of the French people; the German element being — since even the Burgundian stock has been for more than a thousand years subordinately blended with the Gallic—comparatively insignificant, even taking into account one or two other provinces on its borders, of later acquisition; to the ardour and noble egotism of the Keltic mind; and to the grand idea of internal unity which naturally developes itself into a theory of external predominance.

These principles have been uniformly and necessarily prevalent in France, whether, as a Power, it be considered in the earlier periods of its career as feudal, despotic under Louis XIV., democratic under the Convention, or a mixture of autocracy and democracy, as under the Napoleons.

France is unquestionably the index-finger of the European Pentarchy. In almost everything she takes the lead of the Continent, as her natural prerogative, as her uncontested right. Not always the first in invention or in speculative opinions, whether political or philosophical,—but in the practical application of them, in comprehensive but compendious theories respecting them, in deductive reasonings from them,—it is to her as the indicator of civilizing improvements and elevating moral movements that the world will be in all probability indebted for the currency of an idea, and its general adoption. To know the theory of any science or art, social or physical, to be able to estimate its symmetrical proportions and its harmony with others, it is even now necessary to obtain access to French literature. English or German writers will probably give more copious details, and occasionally grander, if somewhat disproportionate, views of particular subdivisions of science, or objects of thought; but nowhere, except under the guidance of the master intellect of France, can the totality of such matters be effectually approached. Along with this completeness, nevertheless, it is conceded, the idea of limit is essentially connected; and so it happens that in some departments of literature the indefiniteness, irregularity, and want of roundness, so to speak, in the Anglo-Teutonic mind, is occasionally productive of a grandeur of effect which all the form and finish of French art, all its constructive and systematic force, fail to accomplish.

The title accorded to her sovereigns, of Eldest

M

Son of the Church, is another proof of this reputation of European leadership pertaining to her by hereditary right; for it requires but little reflection to recognise in this appellation the fact that the early conversion of the Gauls to Christianity was the soundest proof of the superiority of their intelligence over the other subject nations of Rome, and their quick appreciation of all civilizing influences that can possibly be afforded or desired. To this title assumed by her rulers may be added, with at least equal justice, that of the most liberal and enlightened of the national members of the Roman Catholic Church. For though Pepin and Charlemagne were the primal patrons and establishers of the Church in its temporalities, yet from the days of Boniface VIII., and even previously, it is evident that servile submission to the Head of the Church in his secular aspect —for his resemblance to Janus is well-known— rarely or never has formed a feature of French character; while in regard both to doctrinal tenets and ecclesiastical administration, their repeated assertion of what are called the Gallican liberties, is a sufficient vindication of their independent temper, and their just conception of the limits to which even the loftiest human authority is amenable.

The i tical constitution which France at present possesses is the very best she has enjoyed at any period of her history. For anything approaching to a shadow of constitutional government, beyond what may be denominated merely mediæval institutions, such as the *lits de justice* and provincial parliaments, it is only necessary to go back to 1789. The first fatal error committed by the nation, and that from which all subsequent disasters flowed, was the amalgamation of the three orders of the States-General in the one, so-called, National Assembly. True it is that the original deflection of France from her proper orbit was caused by

the perturbing influence of the American revolution, her interference in which was succeeded
by a righteous, but rigid and rapid, retribution
of calamities ; but America, with all its faults,
was prudent enough to avoid that unnatural
desecration of political affinities, which consists
in the forced amalgamation of all orders of
society in one turbulent and ill-assorted assembly. Of the issue of this terribly fierce
republicanism it is needless to recall the recollection, or of the stern and sanguinary period
which succeeded ; or the merely military rule
of the first Empire. The Restoration was a
compromise of forces, material and moral, tra-
ditionary and revolutionary, which eventuated
in a failure more significant to its supporters
than satisfactory to its enemies. The system
inaugurated and perfected by Louis Philippe
was a gross delusion—a mockery of representative government, the fallacy of which was palpable to all, even the populace, at the very

moment they were engaged, with apparently patriotic ardour, in giving it effect. The electoral colleges never numbered much more than a quarter of a million in their lists; while the civil places in the gift of the Crown, or disposable by the Ministry, were upwards of three hundred thousand. In the Chamber of Deputies the King had it mostly his own way; and when he had it not, it was because he cared not. Occasionally, beyond doubt, he found it politic to practise an indifference he possibly might not feel; while at other times, having intrigued successfully with the Opposition to his own Ministry, he would condole, with every appearance of sincerity, with the Cabinet he had himself defeated. Torrents of ministerial eloquence have been known to pour forth at his command, only to be lost in the desert platitudes of predetermined minorities. But this could not last for ever. The system, on the whole, was unsatisfactory to the country. Reforms were desired and proposed, and a popular movement set on foot for securing them. The King unwisely resisted the projected improvements until too late ; and the solemn feast of a Regifugium was a third time celebrated in Paris. The revolution of February followed rather than succeeded. Here again was repeated the monstrous error of a single chamber elected by universal suffrage. Connected with its inglorious career, two only things are known which give to it the slightest degree of interest ; namely, that it was in its defence an ingenious republican general invented the praiseworthy and philanthropic process of effectually nullifying the system of barricades, which had more than once lent to revolution and insurrection a lamentable success never again to be realized ; and that, during a fit of temporary sanity, and in support of the traditional policy of France, succours were despatched to Rome to protect the independence of the Pope. The Assembly, it is sufficient to add, lasted long enough to disappoint every hope that was entertained of it by the real wellwishers of their country; and by the factious conduct of its sections, which refused to unite for any object except to oppose all government, it disgusted the press, which it both restricted and flattered, and affrighted and humiliated France.

It was at this juncture that the President, the elect of the people, who had been elevated to his position by a national vote, comprising a greater number of intelligent voices than ever before recorded in the annals of nations as united for the attainment of a single purpose, took into his own hands the guidance of the state; and subsequently called to imperial power by the same commendatory suffrage, he proceeded at once to solidify the social edifice, shaken and tottering as it was, by a constitution which, if not securing everything that is desirable in national life, is still adapted, with eminent sagacity, to obtain probably the greatest amount of good practicable under the present condition of the society in which it is established.

On the broad base of universal suffrage both the imperial monarchy and the popular representation are founded. If to Englishmen the constitution appears in any point defective, it is in the want of prominence given to the aristocratic element of society. The preservation of the influence proper to each of the great coordinate classes appears essential to the prosperity and stability of a state. It is not enough that the extremes of executive power and democratic opinion be embodied in a government, if the intervening condition supplied by the judgment of an aristocracy be wanting. Rome fell by the absorption of all power in the hands of the Emperors. The Florentine Republic fell by its total exclusion of the aristocracy from their natural share in the government; the Venetian by a like error with regard to the people. But aristocracy and nobility are not the same thing. In England the influence of the intermediate branch of the legislature is wisely provided for. The Peers are even a more highly and widely representative body than the Commons. In France nobility exists, but not aristocracy: as an order, only socially, not politically. The absence of a landed senatorial class, with independent co-ordinate legislative power in the state, is undoubtedly a misfortune ; because such a class, while giving dignity to social traditions and stability to national policy, secures, as far as human prudence can, the treatment of questions both internal and foreign, under conditions totally removed, and equally, from the passing passions of the populace, and from those influences to which from various quarters fluctuating and elective assemblies are always liable. Nor is such an institution necessarily obstructive, further than as deliberation is fortunately preventive of that precipitate success at which the ardour of individual legislators, and even of parties, occasionally aims. The true path of national improvement, and of social and moral elevation, is, like that of all elevations, circuitous. No one ascends a mountain perpendicularly. Earth herself confesses only an oblique inclination to the zenith. If something is lost in the actual enjoyment of a right by the lapse of time, something, on the other hand, is gained in that sense of general security which instinctively accompanies the known unwillingness to change. It is the indirect action of the opinion of the enlightened and reflective minds composing the wealthy and leisured classes of society, and of which this order is the natural interpreter, that eventually decides for good all public questions of importance.

Although, therefore, it is to be regretted that in France this order of the state has not all the perfection attachable to it theoretically, yet the

Senate being composed of members named for life, and comprising many individuals of worth and ability, social eminence, moral influence, and ecclesiastical dignity, it enjoys very sensible advantages over a similar institution in another quarter of the world. A senate should either sit by virtue of its own hereditary and indefeasible right, or by nomination of superior authority. To sit as temporary and accountable delegates of the classes which underlie it socially, but override it politically, is absurd.

But if France be, as has been recently said by an authority of some eminence on matters of that kind, "the most democratic nation in the world," then the revolutionary change which destroyed the old laws of succession to property, and necessitated the subdivision of land in certain degrees of equality among children, was the next best alternative, as the state is now virtually based on a conservative democracy.

This fact, for which neither the English press,

Parliament, nor people has made due allowance, sufficiently accounts for that change in the sentiments of the great body of the French nation towards England, which appears incredible and unintelligible to so many editors, M.P.'s, and colonels of volunteer regiments, who labour so heartily to raise up a feeling of animosity in the people of this country against those who have ceased to return it in kind. The landed proprietary of the country, *i. e.* the people of France, numbering several millions of families, and in a far greater proportion to the total population than our own, as distinguished from the comparatively unsettled, and therefore less responsible, population of the great cities, who are naturally more excitable from being congregated in masses, have come to understand the advantages of a government which wisely but sternly made known its intentions from the day of its accession to be no longer at the mercy of a militant mob perambulating the purlieus of

Paris. These classes were not answerable for the Revolutions of July and February. The revolution for which they are answerable is that of December. And after their experience of what the press and the populace of Paris could effect for and against any government, and for and against each other, their recollection of metropolitan barricades and socialist massacres, both under the auspices of distinguished republican generals, they are scarcely to be blamed for the support of a man in whose elevation they saw the probable realization of a government far superior, at least in strength and moderation, and in attention to the just material interests of the community, to the frightful burlesque then being enacted by the Legislative Assembly. Never was there a more perfect accord between power and opinion. The moment the President and the people came in view of each other they sympathised. Society now, in France, far from being permeated by a despotic rigidity, is rather like the free and fluctuating ocean, which, while capable on the surface of wholesome agitation, and occasionally conflicting currents, is still indisposed, in its interior depths, to disturbance, and in its foundations immoveable. They who inferred, either in England, Germany, or elsewhere, that the elevation of Louis Napoleon to power was a menace to this country, have been simply convicted, by events, of very extensive ignorance. A vagrant princeling, whose sole inheritance was a dream of empire, may be excused referring to his star—they who have nothing else have always their star; and when arraigned before a pompous tribunal, if he spoke of a cause, a principle, a defeat, they were ideas which served to cover with a sort of dignity the issue of a reckless, luckless, bootless expedition. But the responsibilities of power insure a very different style of oratory; and the establishment of the empire has proved from the first the triumph, on the part of France, of an amicable people, a peaceful government, and a policy, in the main, conservative.

Now the great difference between a limited or constitutional monarchy and an autocratic government is, that in one the executive or monarchical authority is responsible, through its ministry, to the representatives of the nation; in the other, the ministry are responsible to the executive power only, by which they are appointed. This is the case in France; and so far, theoretically, it is a despotism. For although the people are truly and efficiently represented, yet the body so returned has no constitutional controlling power over the conduct of the executive. It is certainly useful to the Emperor as an indicative organ of public opinion; and doubtless he duly attends to the signs proceeding from such a source—carefully and conscientiously attends to them, for they are of the utmost importance. But, under these conditions, all the energies of government obviously press in only one direction; and if any considerable accident happens to the state-machine, there is no counterbalancing power provided in the civil constitution able to check the downward rush of things which usually takes place in such circumstances, or steady the ranks and straighten the line of that tumultuous march of events which at such periods may always be anticipated. All the great bodies of state—in fact, the Ministry, the Council, the Senate, the Deputies—are almost merely ramifications or conditions, variously modified, of the executive power.

Now in a very simple state of society, such as mostly prevails under governments inspired by the paternal principle, the course of administration is regulated by a single and unqualified impulse imparted from above; but society under more complicated conditions requires, and indeed naturally generates, a systemized antagonism of interests, by the due friction of whose opposing forces the persistency of progress and the permanent welfare of the community are at once reconciled and secured. Such ought undoubtedly to be the case, it may be said, in France, were one theory of government universally applicable; for, practically, France is the freest country in the world—certain manifestations of political liberty, calculated to imperil public tranquillity, only excepted; and the press may by some be supposed to afford sufficient field for the deployment of these peaceful hostilities among the higher and more refined forces of civilization, to which allusion has been made. But here unfortunately other quantities occur, which, by their mass or their movements, more or less detract from the roundness of the calculation.

In view of the interests of those vastly preponderating classes of the community, the strength of the state, the dominant class, averse

N

to needless change, and opposed to further political experiments at their expense—all, in fact, that may be entitled to claim the national name, —it is not of course to be supposed that these are left without their proper safeguards. These are both negative and positive ; and the first is the Press. The press of Paris, though on the whole conducted with dignity and talent, is not to be taken unreservedly as representative of the opinion of France on all subjects. On questions of domestic national interest, the proprietary masses not seldom look upon it with suspicion or indifference, or, it may be, with hostility. They view indeed with anything but disfavour the warning, prosecution, or extinction of a journal whose obstinate or fatal freedom of speech might possibly prove unfavourable in moments of agitation to the present orderly and prosperous condition of things. An unrestricted press is very well, perhaps— though that has never been known in France,

nor hardly anywhere; but peace, prosperity,
increasing trade, agriculture improving both in
its means and its results, commerce extending,
a revenue unequalled in former periods, unsurpassed in amount, victorious arms, a rectified
position among the nations who once gathered
round her to look with wonder and almost incredulity on the depth of the humiliation to
which she could be reduced—all these are solid
triumphs, substantial prizes, for which France
feels itself indebted to the present government
—any one of which almost might in her eyes
be cheaply bought by the extinction at one
blow of the whole political press. Whether the
press be in fact the vital organ by many supposed, or whether its asserted sensibility and extreme tenacity of life be traceable only to some
old Whig tradition, may perhaps be doubted;
that it will bear, even among Anglo-Saxons,
considerable laceration the moment society feels
itself in want of a strong hand, certain Pre-

sidential amenities practised at New York and other places at the present moment satisfactorily testify. Be this as it may, it is the interests of those vast, sober, frugal, industrious, honest, and hard-living masses of society, with whom the personal and domestic virtues of a Christian people are principally found, which the Imperial Government is both bound and inclined to protect; and which necessarily, in the consideration of all governments,—except perhaps those tentative productions existing in the boundless vacuity of editorial brains, dreaming of the vice-presidentship of provisional administrations, —outweigh a thousand dubious benefits attributable to the mere expression of political speculation, or the petulant discussion of measures deemed advisable by those whose only possible interest is the welfare of the whole nation.

Whatever the degree of representative character, moreover, which the press of Paris may be justified in vindicating for itself, it is certain that from the impulsive nature of the population to which it appeals, its triumphs have always been identical with the overthrow of government, and its subjection and restriction necessary to the normal conditions of civilized and peaceful society. From the excitable character, therefore, of the population of large cities—preeminently, the metropolis—in which political ideas once cast abroad have a tendency to ferment with perilous rapidity before the clearer judgment of the total community has time to be expressed with decision, it is satisfactorily found that the interests of society as a whole are opposed to the unrestrained action of this attractive but dangerous power. To colder constitutions and a more perfectly balanced system like our own, it may, under ordinary circumstances, be harmless; but in France a thoroughly free press has hitherto meant political licentiousness in the widest extent. In the mean time the rural proprietary, the steady masses of the State family, who had never heretofore been consulted or instructed in *la haute politique* of dethroning kings and establishing republics, provisional governments, national workshops, and all that, confess themselves, and very justly, wearied not only of such proceedings, but of all symptoms and tendencies in that direction, such as the political penmen of a metropolitan press too often find it lucrative, in periods of popular commotion, to stimulate. The Imperial Government, it need scarcely be added, has been the only one which, by destroying the anonymous character of the press and wisely rendering its writers individually responsible, has been enabled to reconcile considerable freedom of opinion with administrative energy and social security. And it is in sympathy and compliance with the interests of this vast and almost all-inclusive class that the operation of this institution is felt to require checking so soon as ever it indicates the slightest inclination to pass that boundary mark which the conservators of the public safety have established.

The other safeguard specified as one of a positive nature, is connected with the army. The army, drawn, of course, from those classes recently considered, is a far more really representative institution than the press, and in some respects a substitute for it. A national army and a national press, each in full vigour, can never coexist, unless in a land where military honour is yet to be understood, or where civil rights are not worth having. The press has no ruling idea, if it be not that of total insubordination: it is Babel. In the army, order, discipline, stand for all others. Whatever the original associations of the private—the analytical tendencies of the mind of his officer—there can be no question of the contempt with which the ablest and most exciting article will be conned by a full colonel, intrusted at a perilous time with the preservation of the public peace, nor of the quiet ferocity with which his orders relative to the author, editor, printer, and press, would be executed. This is what is expected of the army as an institution everywhere, and a duty it has been frequently called to fulfil in France.

The conscription is not an invention of imperial tyranny but a republican institution, and is variously regarded as a right to be claimed, as a duty to be discharged, or as a privilege to be desired. The army has been sometimes opposed to the government, and sometimes to the nation. To identify the interests of the army with the stability of the one and the prosperity of the other, the apportionment of France into military districts appears a singularly sagacious precaution. The mere *pronunciamento,* as in former times, of merely one city, or even of one or two provinces, will suffice no longer for the success of any possibly revolutionary movement.

The general opinion of the country must for the
future be consulted, and, more than that, the
general force combined, before the government
could, under any circumstances, be removed
with that somewhat farcical rapidity peculiar
to the trained scene-shifters of the old Parisian
political stage. Whatever contributes to the
security of France, is of the highest interest and
importance both to England and Europe. There
is reason, therefore, for congratulation in the
prospect glanced at. But it is under circumstances of this kind, where so much is dependent
on the will and the skill of a single individual,
that the character and moral tone of one man
becomes, at times, a matter of immense, almost
immeasurable, significance; because such considerations notoriously and seriously influence
the cause of international policy. In this pre-
dicament is the reputation of Napoleon III.
To form a just estimate upon this important
subject, it will be found necessary to assert

either that the events of the time have manifestly belied themselves, or that the British
public generally have been under a false impression; and that the press of this country in particular, always argumentative, never logical,
starting from premisses without foundation,
have committed themselves to conclusions utterly irreconcilable with reason. Let us first
hear the voice of prophecy. The prophets of
our press have predicted, now any time that
can be named during the last ten years, that
Louis Napoleon would embroil all Europe; that
his empire would be the empire of the sword;
that he was bent on avenging Waterloo; that
he would invade England; that he would betray
England some night under cover of a fog; that
he would seize Belgium for the French army,
just to keep their hands warm; that he would
seize the Rhine, probably to cool them; that
he would seize Etruria for his cousin; that he
would seize Sardinia for himself; that he would

snatch Morocco from the jaws of Spain, as
the sea-eagle snatches from the fish-hawk the
prey which an admiring hemisphere was about
to see equitably gorged by the original depre-
dator; finally, that he would seize Syria, in
order that he might figure again, it is to be
supposed, as the Old Man of the Mountain.
None of these things has he done. But far
from being discouraged by this circumstance,
they have been at the trouble to invent for him
a variety of imaginary misdeeds, which it would
be gratuitous cruelty to recapitulate. The
reckless untruths, indeed, uttered upon this
head form one of the most astounding and
melancholy phenomena of the times in which
we live. The fact appears to be this, that
Europe generally during the last ten years has
been at peace; but that in the two wars which
have taken place, one was chiefly at the instigation of England, and in this, along with
France, she took an active part; in the second,

which was commenced by Austria, England gave to France her passive support. In the first case England can boast of having had an ally, and the only one during her long career, whom it was not necessary for her to pay. The sum and value of all the other predictions it were needless to characterise.

But of course there is a cause, even if there be not a reason, for everything. The ostensible cause is the alleged violation by Louis Napoleon of his oath—" *Je le jure* "—to uphold the republican constitution. But it is patent to any one desirous of directing to the matter a calm and clear intelligence adjusted to that point of view in which other considerations connected with the main object show equally clear, that the violation of that oath was a more sacred duty than the keeping of it. Without alluding to proverbial views of propriety in certain cases, it is admitted that it may, and not unfrequently does, become the duty of an individual to forfeit his word, where the change of circumstances has so altered the relative position of the parties to the engagement, that not the most deliberate or sacred vow could require or even justify the literal fulfilment of the contract. Through the mouth of the President the nation no doubt took, as it were, by proxy, the oath at the same moment. But the world knows what the career of the Legislative Assembly proved to be. Never, therefore, was there a more solemn act of absolution, virtually administered by a people who were, and are, the only real judges of the necessity of the case, than when, in those assemblages, comprising much of the opulence, intelligence, and moral worth of the community, which gathered together at all the great points of the President's tour through France, it became manifest that one universal understanding animated the immense masses—not always, it is true, articulate, but always sensible—to the effect that the hour was at hand in which they looked for the total and triumphant abolition of that cumbrous parody of constitutional government over which the man then before them had the misfortune to preside, and under which it was their disgrace, their involuntary disgrace, to live. Never was there a happier or more salutary awakening than that which France was one morning made conscious of, when the spectral and gigantic incubus which so long had weighed upon her tumultuous bosom, at the resolute touch of a stern friend, no longer to be restrained, vanished at one bound into its righteously predestined annihilation. Europe herself, wearied and fevered with watching over that frightful trance, breathed audibly her sense of relief, as each successive symbol and incitement of the pernicious illusion, which had so fatally usurped the faculties of that melancholy but still majestic victim, was by the same strong hand cautiously but unsparingly stripped away ; and while order,

dignity, and power, took the place of turbu-
lence, and weakness, and contempt.

George IV. confessedly violated his oath,
according both to his own and his father's conception of it, when giving his assent to the Bill
for the Emancipation of the Catholics ; and probably no one loved him less on that account—
Lords Winchilsea and Eldon perhaps excepted ;
but few, indeed, considering now the beneficial
consequences of that measure, have looked
with much squeamishness on the transaction :
nay, it will doubtless be sincerely hoped by
many, that if this be his greatest offence, as may
almost be inferred from the lofty virulence
with which a similar act is treated by the purists
of the British press in the case of a contempo-
rary sovereign, even this may ultimately be
forgiven him. The Emperor, moreover, is accused of being a sphinx, whatever that may
amount to ; a false character is attributed to
him, and the complaint spreads that his conduct

is mysterious. He is accused of increasing the army while actually diminishing it; of having the army entirely at his disposal, as if this were not the usual prerogative of the executive; of being entirely himself at the mercy of the army; of ruining the country by the personal extravagances of his court, while France was never so rich, so prosperous, so contented, as at the present moment. So much for prophecy. It might seriously be feared that we are living near the end of the world, or certainly in quite antepenultimate times, since it is written of such periods, that " whether prophesyings, they shall fail;" but that systematic and unexceptional failure leads to a reasonable suspicion of intentional deception. To mislead the public mind by keeping up an eternal alarum that never runs down has been, it must be feared, the intention and the practice of the self-appointed monitor of the people. That the organs of all political parties have coalesced upon this object, proves only, if it proves anything, that the prosperity of the fourth estate is naturally of more importance to itself than the welfare of the third, or the tranquillity of the whole.

So much has been said upon this topic, not only from a due sense of the value of the press as an institution, in which it is obvious, nevertheless, from the necessary operation of natural causes, fear and interest mutually stimulating each other, that public opinion is occasionally at least, on most important matters, refracted rather than reflected; and that by an agitation, which it is its duty to calm and not to exasperate, the objects of national consideration are much too frequently distorted or inverted; but from a conviction that if ever the amicable relations between the two nations are interrupted, such interruption will be traceable to that anonymous, irresponsible, and therefore inconsiderate organ.

The probabilities of such an event are, it is

true, from the close and increasing ties between the two nations, and from the unwonted union of their governments upon questions of foreign policy, daily and happily diminishing. Some few points of divergence, however, it is necessary to touch upon. First, as regards the late war with Russia. In that war England confessedly played a secondary part. The greater number of troops, the greater sacrifice of life, was on the part of the French. The French had, practically, the direction of the hostilities by land. The English were justly to have had the lead in the naval campaign; but it was precisely here that boastful failures were all we could show; and after one or two grand but unsuccessful manœuvres, and just as, it is alleged, our admirals were on the point of exterminating the Russian marine, the Emperor Napoleon accepted proposals of peace. Now if we agree at all to act with allies, it is obviously requisite to look at things with a binocular glass, so as to have one eye for our friends; and the objects of the war being gained, it appeared unwise and unnecessary to prolong it merely for the greater glory of the English naval service; nor was it assuredly to the interest of France or of Europe that the Russian fleet should be annihilated. Various reasons might be assigned to the contrary. But on a comprehensive survey of things, the propriety of the issue adopted can scarcely now be disputed, and indeed is generally acquiesced in; for on the whole it is better that dignity and honour should not be totally lost in any contest by either party.

Alarm has even been sought to be created by a rumour of alliance between France and Russia. But so long as France gives to England her right hand, there can be no objection to her appropriating her left to Russia. The interests of these two Powers in certain matters of continental policy, as distinguished from European, and in which England is not so intimately concerned, run parallel to a considerable extent; in some other matters each approaches nearer to England than the other; but France holds unquestionably the determinative position between the two. Great Britain can never be attacked with effect except by a combination, at the head of which these two Powers must stand; a condition of affairs not very likely to occur. In the mean time France at peace and on terms of amity with Russia, equals, in other words, the quiet of Europe assured.

Between the French and German nations but little affection subsists; and except in literary and scientific circles where individuals of either family have won for themselves by their genius, their labours, or their discoveries, a cosmopolitan renown; and whose achievements for the advantage of mankind are happily viewed

through the colourless light of pure intelligence,—and except in occasional instances of
reciprocal benevolence or social connection,—
their opinion of each other is in fact by no
means daintily disguised or charily expressed;
nor is there much more between Germany and
Russia. But in view of the somewhat debili-
tated condition of Austria, there is a manifest
disposition on the part of France to cultivate
friendly relations with the North of Germany,
and under certain conditions to agree even to
an aggrandisement of Protestant power.

The relations of France with Prussia are
certainly somewhat peculiar. The traditional
assertion by France of the Rhine as her natural
boundary maintains an uneasy feeling in Prussia that still contributes to the good effect of
preventing an open rupture with Austria and
compelling respect to the minor states of Germany. For in any other disposition either the
aid they might solicit would be accorded to

them by France, or the condition she would insist upon would be secured without much trouble.

Now that the struggles of party and the crotchets of individuals respecting the cession of Savoy have ceased, it is plain to every one who reflects upon the matter dispassionately that that province pertains as naturally, and analogously, to France as Monmouthshire to England; considering Wales as representing an independent state. The passes and the slopes of the Alps on her own side unquestionably belong to France; but the truth is that in the day of her humiliation the Great Powers at the Congress of Vienna, considering her probably in the condition of a house to be let, ordered the key to be left at the next door. Whether this was likely to continue when a responsible tenant was once in occupation, may be left to the imagination of even a centaur to discover.

Regarded merely as an infringement of the
treaties of 1815, it is somewhat too late in the
face of such instances as are supplied by Belgium, Cracow, and the generally lauded issue
of the war in Lombardy, to invoke against
France alone the maintenance of public instruments which all the Powers of Europe, greater
and less, have successively lent their hand to
invalidate. France, too, has had her heptarchy
as well as England, and Savoy was the last of
these petty states. As to its being the cradle
of the Sardinian royalty, there is no doubt that
after the conquest of Lombardy the new king
was as content to abandon his cradle as all the
other European dynasties have been. The
cradle of the Hapsburgs, for instance, was in
Switzerland; of the Romanoffs, in Sweden;
of the Hohenzollern, in the township "of that
ilk;" of the Guelphs in Germany; of the Bona-
partes in Corsica. On the other hand it cannot

be denied that the race, the language, the political and commercial interests of the Savoyards were manifestly French; and the real injustice which they suffered was their forced union with a state, from which they were physically divided by a lofty and laborious barrier, which afforded no encouragement for their industry; and in whose representative assembly their own deputies could neither understand the language of their colleagues, nor make themselves intelligible.

The annexation of Nice was a matter clearly distinguishable, in the opinion of many, as a matter of policy and propriety from the former question. Its position, however, between the two nations is analogous to that occupied in our own island by Berwick-upon-Tweed, long the object of contention between two rival kingdoms. The habits and other superficial characteristics of the population, the language chiefly spoken, and the aspects of the city are Italian; but in this case also the more important interests of the city, military and commercial, are undoubtedly French.

With regard to Naples, the conduct of the Emperor of France, far from being, as was asserted, enigmatical, appears perfectly simple and clear. For it is quite certain that in the face of the anti-national farce nicknamed a plebiscito, and which, being theoretically the most solemn and peculiar act of citizenship, seemed to the Piedmontese authorities appropriately and gracefully to be placed under strict military supervision—particularly as the people themselves, those actuated by interest or compulsion excepted, as is evident from the number of votes which amount rather to a deficit than a minority, signalised in most places their opinion by their absence—it is quite clear that for a long time the Emperor, as well as many others anxiously interested in the welfare of the Sicilies, awaited a more direct and trustworthy manifestation of the national will; but seeing that the country was entirely prostrated to the military occupation of Sardinia, and having hitherto in the politest and most complimentary manner forcibly subordinated his policy to that of England on the Neapolitan question, reserving the Roman for himself exclusively, it became obvious that he must in due time withdraw even his fleet from Gaeta unless prepared to demand the withdrawal from Neapolitan territory of the invading troops of his ally. In the mean time those troops increase, and public opinion is totally stifled.

In all speculations current in France upon the Eastern question, Egypt and Syria are intimately involved. French policy has always been to effect the severance of Egypt from the Porte, and secure its independence from even the restrictive jealousy of the tutelary Powers. By her possession of Algeria she has thought to secure its subordination to herself. The canalization of the Isthmus is one means to this end. Anything which tends to increase the importance, increases at the same time the probability of the future independence of Egypt, and such tendency favours the preponderance in Egypt of French influence. French ideas are more prevalent in Egypt than English. Although the commerce of the latter may be much more extensive and has sufficient partisans in commercial quarters, yet the Egyptians believe the English do not take that interest in their general welfare and advancement that the French do, but simply regard them as a territorial convenience for the transit to India of goods and passengers *viâ* Suez. As all contingencies relating to the event before referred to are boldly and unfeelingly alluded to everywhere, it may be affirmed that in the interests of universal commerce the safety of that passage would have to be secured, even if Great Britain should be compelled to add to her known partiality for commanding straits the privilege of fortifying the solitary isthmus in question; and, if the canal should be in existence, of exercising over it the same sublime superintendence which she exercises from her little crater at Aden and her " Rooke's nest" at Gibraltar.

In Syria there is little doubt the French are better liked than ourselves; for, besides their fortunate assumption of the protectorate and championship of the Christians of the Western Church, their exertions are known to have been in favour of the national independence of the natives whether of Mohammedan or other belief. But although the Arabs hate the Turks passing well, and although it may be opined that should the latter ever be expelled from Europe—and they could not be expelled from everywhere—they would probably in such case centralise their power round Damascus or Jerusalem, it is not certain which of these races would be most obnoxious to the French, who have, like ourselves, their own national weakness—an undisguised propensity for the occupation of foreign capitals, the seats and centres of ancient civilisation and historic renown.

In Further India France is apparently following a plan which, as with England in the dominions of the Mogul, will likely end in the subjugation gradual but total of immense territories. In China the policy of France has been entirely subsidiary to our own, which ever since the opium war may be, in the opinion of many honourable men now, and possibly will be by impartial history, characterised as one unequalled, unvaried, unmitigated iniquity;—an iniquity now shared by our allies, who with ourselves have appropriately closed our political relations with the Celestials—who, whatever their claim to that title will be ready enough to apply to us its opposite—by an act of wanton barbarism, devastation, and outrage, associated

for ever with a name now known from the
Ægæan to the Pacific, as synonymous with
a passionate regard for all that is venerable
in art, or beautiful in its combination with
nature.

Much has been said and written concerning
the augmentation during late years of the
French navy ; but there does not appear to be
anything in this fact, rightly considered, to
arouse the hostility or the jealousy of England.
After the long and disastrous naval war in which
the marine of France had been notoriously reduced to a very low and inadequate condition,
but little attention was paid to it during the
reigns of Louis XVIII. and Charles X. After
the accession of the Orleans line, a Report,
sanctioned and headed by the Prince de Join-
ville, was made to the Government, recom-
mending an immediate and continual increase,
calculated to extend over at least the twenty
years succeeding, of that branch of the warlike

forces of the State. The recommendation was adopted by the republic, and has been simply continued by the Emperor. And if it be borne in mind that a just proportion is requisite to be maintained between the two arms into which the material forces of a State requiring both means of defence are divided, it is necessary also to remember that France has, in addition, another law of proportion to observe—namely, that if England takes of right the headship of the world in this matter, France, with the largest and most important seaboard of any nation in Europe, feels herself perfectly justified, there can be no question, in assuming as her proper station, in point of naval strength, the lead of the continental Powers. Nor has she, nor has Europe forgotten, that during the Crimean war France was compelled to borrow of England the means of conveyance for some thousands of her troops; a circumstance which it is quite certain, from the tone adopted towards her recently by the English Parliament and press, she would not wish to see repeated; and any future necessity for which it is her just object to avoid.

GREAT BRITAIN.

GREAT BRITAIN.

Of all countries England is the most truly representative, not only socially with regard to races, but constitutionally with regard to principles of government. Comprising within her moderate limits a more notable variety of race than in a similar space can be found in any single State, she is consciously productive of their combined virtues and distinguishing characteristics. There is an absolutism in this country more perfect than that obtained under any despotic Power of Europe, but it is the absolutism of law; there is a democracy, more honourable to the advancing intelligence of the world than either Athens of old or New York

in modern times has furnished as an example
to history, for it is the only democracy that has
proved itself reasonable. Where constitutional
freedom, the crown of the subject, is held in
reverence by an executive, still conscious that
the eye of liberty has ere now tamed the lion-
like glare of even royal prerogative, and where,
at the same time, loyalty to the sovereign, like
a law of nature, unwrit but universal, pervades
all classes of society, there is necessarily attained
and exemplified the perfection of civil government.   It is true this has been achieved only
by stern, laborious, and painful processes; so
much so that Englishmen frequently feel a kind
of incredulous contempt for nations who have
essayed or who desire to occupy a position commanding similar immunities, without sufficiently
dignifying themselves by preparatory sufferings.
And in this there is some reason.   This mental
attitude is indicative of a certain mastery
achieved—of a certain truth realized.   It may

be doubted whether a simultaneous upheaval of the political surface of all nations to one level would be desirable, were it possible. The constitutions of nations are almost as various as the productions of nature ; and while, materially, the populations flourish by the cultivation and interchange of their own peculiar produce,—their political welfare, it is also apparent, is better secured by each one striving to perfect its appropriate institutions than by vainly endeavouring to naturalise others of an alien growth, and perhaps uncongenial habit. These institutions it is pretty safe to consider in the light of political optimism, and at periods of ordinary quiescence as not far from the best applicable to their possessors. Exact uniformity of government is not only, of course, impossible, but it may be credited that even a very near resemblance is undesirable. Uniformity is always dear to despotism ; and now that the sanction of Divine authority is so ready to be propounded in favour of every autocratic government, the greater the varieties by which communities are demarked the better; for variety involves, more or less, covert antagonism; antagonism, self-reliance; self-reliance, safety.

It is undoubtedly an advantage to a State to have a clear and definite line of policy; so that not only its own principles and practice may coincide, but that other nations may know what it is prepared to do—what to defend, and to shape accordingly their own course. Up to the close of the great revolutionary war in 1815, this was manifestly the case with Great Britain. The supremacy of the seas and the independence of the continental nations, as opposed to the aggressive domination of France, were the objects for which she strove, and which to a certain extent, in concert with others, she gained. This was a conservative policy. From the period immediately succeeding, owing to the cessation of war and the introversion of the national mind exclusively on its own domestic affairs, a great reaction took place; and during the next ten years, under the auspices of Mr. Canning, who seemed more ambitious to make a great name than to guide consistently the course of government, a policy was adopted of a nominally liberal character, calculated apparently to undo almost all that his country had been labouring to establish previously. Because France was still suspected—that is, within five years of her complete overthrow—of ambitious views towards the Pyrenees, Mr. Canning conceived the brilliant idea of effectually preventing the realization of any such designs by stripping Spain of the best means of support she had, not only against France individually, but of maintaining a superior position among the nations of Europe generally. So, to spite France, he humbled Spain. "If France," said Mr. Canning, "is to get possession of Spain, it shall not be Spain with the Indies." Thus, although the

alleged intention on the part of France was
never proved, and although nothing has ever
transpired to warrant the idea that it was entertained,—her action in Spanish affairs being
repressive, not aggressive,—all the American
colonies of Spain were encouraged, instigated,
stimulated, to revolt, and the expenses of their
respective revolutions generously paid for by the
people of this country. Led by a Conservative
minister of Liberal leanings, Englishmen appear
to have believed, without examination, reflection, or forethought, that revolutions were the
most natural expression of popular sentiment;
and that peace, progress, prosperity, general enlightenment, wise legislation, with no hostilities
more sanguinary than rival arguments might
furnish to conflicting politicians, were confi-
dently to be looked for from a people so eager
to secure the enjoyment of public rights and
national independence. Debts, it was urged,
were easy to be discharged where an unlimited

supply of silver was to be had for merely mining. The independence of the colonies was proclaimed; and what has been the result? Have they redressed, as the eloquent minister announced, the balance of the Old World? or rather, while the mother-country has been slowly but perceptibly improving for many years, have not her degenerate offspring been as sensibly receding into a lawless, unprincipled, denationalized condition? Misled by false notions of the value of political liberalism, and taking no security for the just influence of station and property, and the consecration and elevation of law, it has been the policy of this country notably in recent times— and of the United States uniformly and naturally, because their diplomatists knew what lay before them—to support every successive change of government that promised more liberality than its rival. But it is not liberality that society wants in such conditions; it is stability.

Mexico, in little more than thirty years, has passed through every form of which mis-government is capable, from military monarchy to perfect anarchy. An armed faction enters, say by the south, a certain town, which it squeezes like an orange, and departs; the following day a hostile band enters by the north, and pares it to the core. Doubtless the major part of the Mexican people, at the present moment, to judge from the satisfaction exhibited during recent events by the inhabitants of Hayti, would be glad enough to be taken again under the old dominion. In the mean time France, Spain, and England, having each their separate and crying grievance against this wilful, worthless, and incompetent creation—the triumph of British liberalism, are unitedly despatching a force, both military and naval, to Mexico, not of necessity for the purposes of war, but of a certainty to administer a just reproof, by taking from her the control of some portion of those resources which she has so long neglected or so industriously misapplied, and directing them to more honest and useful ends. If injudicious counsels on her part should unhappily render direct hostilities necessary, still it must be confessed that as in this case there cannot be a scruple of doubt as to which party is in the right and which in the wrong, warlike measures may be sometimes viewed as the expression of the reason of a nation; as it is not unfrequently more rational to effect an object by force than waste the world's time by a vain appeal to unappreciated arguments.

That England should have employed her influence in such a manner as only to bring about a state of things in which revolution and insurrection constitute the normal state of society—where the only hope of the peaceable, the orderly, and the industrious, lies in the administration of martial law, and where insult and injury to their main benefactors have become a national custom—is a fact much to be deplored, and can only be accounted · for on the understanding that liberalism is a principle too vague to supply a distinct policy, except at the expense of its own consistency.

By the same species of policy it is, nevertheless, only fair to admit the independence of Greece and of Belgium was subsequently effected ; but care was taken in those cases to provide a more compact and duly graduated political system, the result of which has been so far and on the whole satisfactory.

But since the great contest between the aristocratic and democratic parties in this country, which was closed by the passing of the Reform Act—a wise, just, and wholesome measure in itself—the popular feeling and the Government, or rather the successive Administrations, naturally affected by it and the urgent adjurations of the press, have tended perpetually and with increasing velocity to a policy that can only be described as "amateur insurrectionist." Wherever tidings arrive of a hostile feeling to any government, of a threatening movement, of an incipient agitation in any quarter of the world— Ireland, India, and the Ionian Isles excepted— to that quarter our sympathies are immediately directed—though as destitute, it may be, of all true direction as the gyrations of the needle in a tropical storm—and loudly and unmistakeably expressed. Whether such ought to be the conduct of this country, and whether we are acting in a worthy or dignified manner, or on a principle we should approve of as applied to ourselves, a very little reflection on the present course of things will enable an impartial judgment summarily to decide.

In the solution of many important political questions which mainly affect particular States in certain relations, England, by means of her vast social activity, public discussion, and open press, will always be found to have a direct interest, if only of an internal character; for it is the speculative opinions of multitudes, or of eminent individuals on these points, which demark parties and decide the incidence of policy. The greater, of course, is the necessity in such matters both of caution and consistency.

With regard to the resuscitation of extinct nationalities, for which the aid and sympathy of Great Britain are so often invoked, it may be worth while in the first place to ask ourselves the question whether any combination of forces, territorial, general, or religious, in presence of the virtual council of Powers which presides over the international affairs of Europe, could effect upon the whole a more just or safe equilibrium of interests than that which at present exists? A negative answer will, it is strongly suspected, be found necessary.

The resuscitation of Poland is one of these political problems which, like perpetual motion

—on the theory that everything that is possible
has a comparative degree of probability, hangs
upon men's minds with a kind of uncouth
fascination, which is only lamentable when
they remember that at the time of its first
division England was squabbling with Spain
about the Falkland Islands; and at its second,
occupied in barren hostilities with France
about the possession of Corsica. And supposing Poland made independent, does it
not occur that a vast deal might be said by
sympathetic Poles in favour of reviving the
extinct kingdom of Wales? Did not his late
majesty King Edward, of glorious memory, per-
petrate unheard-of enormities in the reduction
of that ancient and illustrious nation—a nation
possessing its own laws, literature, social institutions of the very freest character, perfect
independence, a long line of kings and sages
whose pedigrees of thousands of years are still
preserved, and in some cases perpetuated to

the present day ?   And what could a barbarous
Power like England say in reply?

Russia is troubled with Poland.   The universal press of this country immediately adopts
the cause of Poland.   Nothing appears so probable from the temper of the democratic party
in Europe at the present hour as that an
attempt will be made to effect the resuscitation
of Poland; and although the moral assistance
of France, who has too long played the part
of a disturber of nations, and of England may
be assumed, nothing appears so unlikely to
succeed; and if we consider that that event
implies the successive or simultaneous overthrow of the military power of two empires and
one great Protestant kingdom; and when it
is remembered that the establishment of the
latter was acquiesced in by England at the
time, principally as forming a counterpoise
to the oppressive influence throughout the
Continent, of the Germanic Empire ; and

that the effect of such a change would be the foundation of another Catholic Power as a member of the great European Council of States, it may be seriously doubted what would be the ultimate gain to society in the sum of constitutional government or moral and intellectual liberty.

Hungary is a trouble to Austria. Immediately our publicists, many members of Parliament, many provincial leaders of public opinion, and others, issue or deliver stirring appeals to the British people in favour of Hungary as an independent Power. Enough has probably been said upon this question. It remains only to add that in their last movement the Hungarians have plainly taken up a position where they will inevitably find themselves on the exhausted side of the process. When passive resistance ends in the voluntary abnegation of all government and machinery of administration among a people, the wisdom of such a course, or the sublimity of such a spectacle becomes very doubtful; especially when it is remembered that this is done in a country not of backwoods or deserts, where it might be difficult to supply another administrative body on the moment; but that side by side with it is a government from the highest to the lowest offices duly organised and prepared to fill up immediately every vacant place that occurs. Such conduct looks more like fatuity than anything else.

But has Hungary any grievance to complain of which our Hungary would not be glad to adopt by exchange for some of her own? Do both complain that they are prohibited from public meetings of a political character, and from bearing arms, the distinctive ensigns of freemen, which every boy in England or Scotland may bear? Yet which of them is it that has to complain of the last insult that can be offered to a subjected state, their compulsory support of a religion which is in their eyes odious and heretical?—a mark of thoughtful and humane legislation by which one of the poorest peoples in Europe are called to pay twice over for the exercise of their religious duties,—a proof of civil and national equality which would be in England unendurable, in Scotland unattemptable. Which of them is it that has to complain that a barbarous outrage on the rights of humanity, in which old men, women, and children were turned out roofless from their homes on the bleak hillside; which, if a specimen of episcopal Christianity, is carefully to be distinguished from the hospitable duties enjoined on the Christian episcopacy; and which if it had occurred in the steppes of Russia, or the sands of Africa, or the forests of Brazil, would have called forth indignation meetings in almost every town in England, only happening in Ireland, moved not our sympathy at all? It moved not the less, let us remember, the sympathy of France. It moves not the less the kindly jeers of Austria at British inconsistency.

It may not be denied that a distinction is to be drawn between the policy advocated by the public organs of opinion and the policy found practicable by Government; for Governments are responsible not only to their respective peoples but to the free opinion of other Governments, and of the world generally. But in consequence of this inconsistency—and many a home truth is administered in despatches which if seen at all by a discerning public it is fain to admire in the shape of blanks and asterisks—the Government of this country has lately almost confined itself to the so-called policy of non-intervention. This, if honestly carried out, may be as justifiable in certain cases as any other. But non-intervention in case of a flagrant invasion of another's rights may be as radically base as the offence itself;

and as utterly impolitic as can be conceived. And again, non-intervention which is intervention under a disguised name, which is in fact sub-intervention, can be neither honest nor in any way satisfactory. If indeed non-intervention loses its genuine character of wise impartiality and entire abstinence, it may prove both wrong and injudicious in any indefinite degree.

Attention has been previously directed to Italy. The eyes of the world are still upon her. Great Britain, adopting nominally this principle —if such it can be called—of non-intervention, has been aiding and abetting Sardinia in her attack upon the kingdom of the Two Sicilies. First, let it be shown with what means; and secondly, with what results. At the outset it was decided that our moral assistance was to be accorded. But of course, as that did not amount to much, certain legal authorities were fortunate enough to discover, whether in Vattel or Blackstone does not appear, that moral aid meant volunteer forces, of which the Government were supposed not to know. However impressive may be the effect under the most solemn circumstances of "winking Virgins," it cannot be denied that this must have been at least rivalled in the emphatic operations performed by the nictitating membranes of certain official dignitaries at that time in our House of Commons.

Now volunteer forces such as these were—and their composition need not be characterised—despatched abroad, appear open to every possible objection. They are unsatisfactory generally to the people desiring aid ; they are ill-assorted, ill-regulated, wanting in that common bond and *esprit de corps* which is the foundation of military companionship and military honour ; and in fact they are mostly no better than the lowest class of mercenaries, mere *condottieri*. The Government that permitted them is not responsible for their conduct ; and at the same time the Government accepting their assistance has not the direct control over them; being hampered partly by unwillingness to incur the displeasure of a friendly people, and other considerations, when correction and example might be reasonably required. These considerations were thoroughly exemplified in the conduct of those who so worthily represented England in the hostilities which took place at Naples; and which induced the great volunteer himself, their leader, to exclaim, no doubt with the heartiest honesty, when quitting the country, "Thank God! I have done with the British volunteers!"

It becomes a great nation either to engage in war, if it should prove unavoidable, avowedly, and for the recognised purposes of war; or to keep peace altogether. But this peddling, shuffling, underhanded, amateur revolutionism is equally opposed to honour and to common sense.

The results, in the next place, of this policy,

in which it must be admitted that the Government and the public frankly and wholly coincided, may be worth considering. France, by her superior weight and activity, intelligence, and material resources, by all the sympathies of the Gallo-Roman race, of which she is the head, with its subdivision of Kelt and Iberian, by identity of religion and contiguity of position, draws irresistibly along with her wherever she may tend, both Spain and Belgium. To these may now be added virtually Italy. In case of a general war, such as Europe has once seen, none of these separately could resist; they must therefore in all probability be looked upon as her subordinate allies. In case of a war between England and France, which would be partly carried on in the Mediterranean, Italy, exposed to invasion as she is by France, must speedily choose her side; and which that must be, her geographical position and various other considerations leave no room for conjecture. It is necessary to go back for a year or two. When the war undertaken by the Emperor of France which issued in the independence of ˌNorthern Italy, and when, by the absorption of Tuscany and the other duchies into the Sardinian dominions, the undue preponderance of Austria in the Peninsula was done away, and for the future effectually guarded against, the Emperor had obviously fulfilled the pledges indicated in his expression of "freeing Italy from the Alps to the Adriatic." For he had no wish, it is manifest, either to destroy the kingdom of Naples, or to render Italy one kingdom; which was an event precipitated, contrary to his own views, by the ambition of Count Cavour; and as yet only nominally realised. It may be that France was not desirous to see an united Italy. But whether that be or be not the case, it is here where England may very possibly feel first the consequences of the derangement of the balance effected by the recent innovation, if it proves of sufficient strength to perpetuate itself.

But seeing that the northern part of Italy, having broken from Austria, has become attached to France, and will indeed always be subsidiary to that Power, it would have only appeared reasonable that England should have desired to see the southern portion of the peninsula in an independent condition. A few years ago Naples was at all events a rival of, and might have been at any time a check to, Sardinia, with an equal army and a superior fleet; and the Government and people attached to us, and England to them by mutual favours and reciprocal gratitude,—England always acknowledging the immense utility on a former occasion which the ports of that Power, when friendly, were to her. But now all these conditions are reversed, and the whole weight of benefit, past and prospective, is transferred to France, whose policy it has always been to extend her influence over all the Mediterranean States. In this we have been generously aiding her. But suppose Italy arrayed against her, what would be likely to become of Sardinia then, with the finest harbour in the Mediterranean, and its inviting position between Corsica and Algeria?

Such have been and are likely to be the effects of a supposed liberal policy towards Naples,—a policy which is entirely independent of the question whether Ferdinand was despotically inclined, or whether the administration of the laws was not grossly abused. The withdrawal of the constitutions granted to Naples and Sicily at different times by Ferdinand and his father was, it must be understood, a compulsory act, for which history witnesses, on their part, that the Austrian Government was responsible; and which certainly in any just view of things cannot be brought forward as a plea for the dethronement of their successor. His faith was unimpeached, his personal conduct was irreproachable; he had only just succeeded to the crown, when his dominions were surreptitiously and unwarrantably attacked by a horde of vagrant adventurers from every country, and an ominously disproportioned contingent of deserters from almost every army in Europe. Surrounded by treacherous advisers and an incompetent ministry, he had had neither time to mature nor opportunity to prepare organic improvements in the constitution, while Italy was still vibrating from the shock of war. The constitution, nevertheless, which in spite of ministerial treachery and incapacity—in spite of the poltroonery of an army which surrendered at the discharge of a *feu de joie*, and of a navy which sold itself to the enemy in the sight of its sovereign—the King did offer to his country, was at least as liberal as that which is found so satisfactory in Sardinia. But this was refused, on the plea that it also might be withdrawn. The worthlessness of this plea is manifest, as well as the fact that the refusal was instigated at Turin, from the consideration that Austrian influence being no longer to be feared, it depended solely upon the people themselves whether they thought proper or not to guard and give effect to their most cherished rights. Possibly the character of our own King John was not all that his people wished; but they having once got hold of their Magna Charta were quite willing to accept the responsibility of seeing it duly executed. It rested entirely with the Neapolitans themselves whether this constitution remained a dead letter or not. But the people, bewildered by the glamour of a romantic outrage and a brilliant atrocity, signed away their heritage among the ranks of royal nations to accept at the hands of a guerilla captain the position of a state discrowned, and a subjugated and insulted province.

In this condition they remain for the present, bitterly but hopelessly repentant, while no fewer

than six Royal Lieutenants in twenty months
have testified to the grateful enthusiasm with
which the Sardinian authority has been accepted; and no fewer than sixty thousand
troops, under the leadership of a man distinguished for severity of discipline, are necessary
to moderate the transports of the people at the
sight of their Piedmontese deliverers.

It can hardly be disputed that the influence
of all regularly-organised States, as any government is better than anarchy, ought naturally
to be exerted rather in favour of amending such
institutions, whether native or foreign, as require it, than in destroying, or in permitting
them to be wantonly destroyed, whether by
internal insurrection or outward attack.   If,
therefore, instead of abiding by this dubious
principle of non-intervention where a wrong was
being openly perpetrated before their eyes, the
two great Powers, truly liberal but justly conservative, had distinctly said, "We will not

allow this outrage to proceed at the instigation of a rapacious monarch and a mendacious minister; but if the population of these countries be desirous, as they doubtless and with reason are, of a free constitution, we take it upon us, with their consent, in the event of their not being able to enforce the observance of it against any attempted fraud or force on the part of the royal authority, to guarantee it as effectually at least as the Austrians formerly ensured the despotic government of the kingdom," the people would have been satisfied, the independent authority of the state preserved, harmony between the national institutions secured, and an honourable, consistent, and judicious policy justified. For after all, good government is a far more important matter than theoretic unity. Nor are all unions happy or fortunate; witness the union of Kolmar : while that of England and Scotland, so often appealed to, was effected not by force, but hereditary succession.

Let a moment's regard be now paid to the Papacy. Viewed territorially or politically, the Papal States occupy the innermost ring of a series of concentric circles, the first of which comprises its nearest neighbours, Sardinia and Naples; the next Austria, France, and Spain, all of which are Catholic Powers; the outermost embraces England, Prussia, Protestant Germany, Scandinavia, and Russia, the great heretical Powers of Northern Europe. So far from Rome being considered as essentially opposed to civilizing influences, it must be admitted that Rome is the original ganglion of intellectual Europe, and that to her the continent at large is indebted mainly for its religion, laws, civilization, and much of its art and literature. The Pope is primarily a spiritual, secondarily a temporal sovereign. In Catholic countries, whatever their constitution, he exercises a subordinate authority. In Protestant States, especially our own, the sovereign authority is primarily of a temporal character; in a secondary sense, of a spiritual. There is no reason to be found in the nature of things why instances of each order should not be compatible with good government. But there are considerable parties in all states who are not only always anxious for change, but chronically indisposed towards any particular government under which they may happen to live. The present Pope signalised his advent to the Pontificate by establishing a liberal and secular administration of the temporal affairs of his dominions, provided for by a senate, which, with nearly a hundred members, comprised only four ecclesiastics; but because he did not march fast enough with the democratic tendencies of an extreme section of his subjects—because he would not consent to the inconsistency of declaring war against the Austrian empire, which no sane man, in his position, could be expected to do—his minister, Count Rossi, a man of

liberal, enlightened views, in favour of a substantial but moderate amount of popular control over public affairs, was brutally assassinated
on the steps of the Senate-house; and His
Holiness himself besieged in his palace, and
finally compelled to exile himself from the
scene of his benevolent but ill-met exertions.
The Rome of the republican revolutionists followed; and quickly, but by no means too soon,
came to an end. Since that time, as might
naturally be expected, but little encouragement
existed among the better-informed and peace-
ably-disposed inhabitants of the Roman States,
to induce them to persuade the Pope to repeat
his former experiment. The state, moreover,
of Italy generally has been such as to present
but few available opportunities of such an
attempt being made. Nor can it ever be made
until Sardinia has definitively abandoned her
senseless and outrageous ambition, and, content
with the very considerable accessions to her

dominion, which she has already acquired in the north of the Peninsula, leaves her southern neighbours in the peaceable enjoyment of their just rights. A threefold division only can be looked forward to as a permanent arrangement of Italian affairs. The unity of Italy is, it is almost unnecessary to say, a delusion, which, even if forcibly effected for a season, could not probably long endure. It is contrary to the interests of the Catholic world that the Head of their Church should be dependent on another Power. The Pope cannot be a subject. Nor can there be any reasonable doubt of the views entertained on this matter by the most important personage connected with it, and who is as intimately acquainted with the necessities as he is interested in the prosperity of the Catholic Church. It must indeed be apparent to all, that the interests of Catholicism generally would emphatically dictate the propriety of preserving the Head of that religion, which succeeds to power by election, independent in the matter of temporalities ; neither seeking aggrandisement nor dreading diminution, nor covertly soliciting subsidies nor active aid from rivals in its favour ; and it seems very doubtful whether the internal harmony of even nominally heretic States would be increased by the threatened destruction of the Papacy as an European sovereignty. Religious institutions are all of a conservative character, whether viewed in their doctrinal or administrative capacity. Religious influences are progressive only in the individual, and expansible solely in the direction of the spirit of interpretation.

England, it is true, has no precise policy towards the Papacy, having no direct relations with it. But the current, or rather the torrent, of public opinion has been manifestly, on all sides, in favour of its total demolition as a temporal power. Many, including some Catholics, who are desirous of such an event, have doubt-

less reasons satisfactory to themselves to ad-
duce ; but that the Conservative party should
join the cry, or even Liberal supporters of Church
and State adopt it, seems scarcely reasonable :
for in this very measure, so desired and lauded,
is obviously involved the principle of all Church-
temporalities, whether pertaining to the Episcopacy or the minor dignities of our ecclesiastical
system ; and they who have a Pope in every
parish, originally endowed with such temporalities as he enjoys under the auspices of some
mediæval Papal potentate, might rationally
request him to hesitate a moment before he
altogether sanctions the vote for the deposition
of his illustrious prototype. For the democratic
party, already, perhaps, preparing its plans in
secret, and maturing an eventual and inevitable
triumph, will not be slow to adopt a precedent at
once so ready and appropriate. The argument
may run thus, by easy stages :—The Head of
the Catholic Church, the Bishop of Rome, does

not require temporalities; neither, of course, does any minor Bishop. The Roman Catholic Bishops in a Protestant country, say England, require no temporalities. Why should a Protestant Bishop in a Roman Catholic country, say Ireland? Why even a Protestant Bishop in a Protestant country? Let us begin with the secularization of all Church property, and let every priest, as in France, whatever his persuasion, be paid by the State a just stipend, graduated according to his titular dignity. These are the known views of the advanced school of democrats; and it behoves all cautious men to beware how they play into their hands even for the gratification of an almost national animosity. For if in the political turmoil of the present times such a movement as is now on foot should by haphazard succeed, and if at any time the revenues of the Church fall into the hands of the vanguard of democracy, the ecclesiastical dignitaries of all establishments and of all grades may perhaps regret, when too late, their ill-omened triumph over His Beatitude, the Pope of Rome. The great body of English Dissenters swell, as might be expected from .their antagonism to State churches, the outcry against Rome; but Dissent is also as good as established by law, and has likewise its endowments.

But the kingdom of Italy, it is said, is an accomplished fact, and all that any one has to do is to put up prayers for its long continuance and prosperity. Let it be so assumed. There is a tendency of the times to accept all acknowledged facts, whether arising from piety, indifference, or criminal complicity with the actors, as events illustrative of the Providential administration of mundane affairs; and since it would be absurd to charge prophets with presumption, it will be advisable in those who think otherwise, to suspend the controversy until some decisive confirmation, in the shape of national or general advantage, may have accrued, or an

appropriate rectification unmistakeably desig-
nated the finality of perfect justice ; for such is
the most tangible and least fallible test by
which is manifested the accordance of any event
with Divine decrees.

In the mean time, although it is distinctly
within the modern historic period that the
Cantons of Switzerland were seen, like moun-
tains from the waters of the Flood, slowly and
one by one emerging from the obscurity of un-
recognised existence, to open and majestic welcome as a sovereign State among the brotherhood of independent nations, yet neither is it
often that the very " *incunabula gentis* " have
been so closely observed nor so patently displayed through the many complicated processes
of diplomacy and war, as in the case of the
Italian kingdom. For although it could not be
proved that the kingdom of Italy, like that of
Rome, was founded upon open violence and un-
measured falsehood ; like that of Carthage, on

consummate treachery and more than Machia-
vellian perfidy; like that of Macedon, on the
reckless infringement of all national treaties,
all rights, all courtesies of friendly governments; like one that shall be nameless, on a
plot which an European statesman would have
hesitated to believe capable of conception by
even a renegade Vizier: yet indications, it is
to be feared, both of force and fraud, as is too
probably the case in the early histories of all
nations, have somewhat gloomily illuminated
the initials of her career.

It will be fortunate, indeed, for some yet
living, and still more for the memory of others
now gone, if circumstances such as these should
prove able to vindicate for themselves successful exemption from a fate consecrated by
the almost universal experience of humanity in
every age; for otherwise, to the shadowy sove-
reignties of Cyprus and Jerusalem, already so
productive and enjoyable to the ambitious House

of Savoy, may be added the equally misty magnificence of the royalty of Italy.

The relations of Great Britain to America at the present moment naturally occupy the general mind. In the war now raging between the elder and younger of the two governments into which the late United States are practically divided, the elder assumes that our sympathies ought to be directed exclusively to herself. But it somewhat strangely happens that England sympathises with both, and can yet conscientiously decline to assist either. The American contest does not represent a single question only, but rather a chain of questions. Take first the view of the Union politically. The North has always talked aggressively of Canada; the South, of Mexico, Cuba, and the British West Indies. But by the disunion these questions, if not absolutely dismissed from all apprehension, are deferred indefinitely. By disunion the two Powers are calculated beneficially to moderate each other's proceedings, and to render impossible for the future any such things as Ostend manifestoes. Nor would there be any cause for regret in such a circumstance to Americans themselves—nothing that would be inimical to their vast and destined progress. But progress is as different a thing as possible from conquest. The balance of power was, in fact, needed in America as distinctly as it is in Europe.

In the commercial view of the question, the North, it may be said, has succeeded for many years in establishing for its exclusive benefit a high protective tariff, of which the Southern States were directly, and Great Britain indirectly, the appointed victims. This protective system of the Northern manufacturers formed the only important question, besides Slavery, upon which a libration of internal interests could be established; and the twin lobes of the national brain—their Parliament and their Press

—discharge the perpetually accumulating batteries of thought and sentiment by which they were supplied from the entire system of the body politic. For whether on the summit of the mountain, or the side of the sea, or the heart of the forest, these questions everywhere confronted each other. Both these questions had long ago arrived at maturity. It was time their claims should be settled; they were incompatible with—indeed they were insufferable of—each other; and it had long been evident that no settlement, short of that to be effected by an armed struggle, could be satisfactory. That struggle, still pending, is partly a contest of race. Commercially, there can be no doubt England sympathises with the South, both in the abstract and in the practical view of the matter of Free Trade; for, with us, it involves the material welfare of millions engaged in manufacture, and indeed the general prosperity of the country.

Socially, again, there can be no doubt that our national regard towards the two great antagonists is about equally divided; for one is fighting for unity of dominion, concerning which a kind of craze has pervaded political circles in England and Europe generally during the last few years; and the other for independence; and though this appears to a judicial mind an object, in a moral point of view, at least equally worthy with the other, yet considerations connected with physical and superficial aspects of things attract, as might be expected, a more numerous class of supporters.

But, morally, there exists another and deeper cause of antagonism between the elder and younger Powers, in which, it must be confessed, neither is sufficiently humane or sincere to secure the unqualified moral support of England. Even the extreme Abolition party in the North do not stand upon the same platform as England in reference to this question. They have neither made the same sacrifices, nor shown the same disposition to meet the legitimate consequences of the sacrifice when made. Either the coloured classes, for instance, must be treated with consideration socially, and some approach to civil equality, or emancipation is a mockery. A people which refuses to eat, drink, sit, walk, talk, or worship with another does so either because naturally and justly superior to the other, or because they are hostile. For if equal, why endeavour to effect a theoretic level which practically you will not recognise? If friendly, why assume such a repulsive and repressive attitude?

But the truth is, there is insincerity on both sides; for while one endeavours to justify practical inhumanity as an alleged necessary element of the institution, the other asserts the institution itself to be incapable of reconcilement with Christianity, or piety indeed of any description. In this view of the case, it need scarcely be added, the religious public of England unanimously coincide. But they who have listened—true, these are not many—to the arguments of any serious and intelligent Southerner on this matter, have some difficulty in subscribing unconditionally to this, even when dignified by the circumstance of its being known to be the John Bull view of the question. "If Abraham," he says, "and all the Hebrew patriarchs possessed slaves, the fact of ownership cannot be considered as absolutely incompatible with personal piety or acceptance with Deity. In the Gospels, though the word slave is repeatedly introduced, slavery is never denounced as an institution by the Saviour; and although the English translation uses invariably the word servant, yet the Greek *doulos*, if meaning anything, certainly means slave. So too, it may be said by the way, with the Latin *servus*. All words indicative of a diminished force in the original idea of servitude, which was slavery,

and suitable indeed to the artificial delicacy of
modern life, and the intricate classification of
existing society, are, so to speak, transparent
shadows of expression, which the ancients, if
ever, rarely, and the writers of the Sacred
Volume never, studied or attempted to convey.
But in the Pauline Epistles undoubtedly is the
most critical authority to be found for the regulation of opinion among Christians upon this
institution. Now Paul, unlike the remainder
of his apostolic brethren, was, in all likelihood,
born a gentleman; speaking of him, therefore,
in his unregenerate days, it may be allowable to
say of him that he had received the advantages
not only of private tuition, but of a university
education; he might have been called, by an
approximation to our modes of speech, a Tarsus
man, or a Tarsonian; he had read the Greek
dramatists, and had probably been present at the
Olympic Games; he had seen something of the
world; he had travelled considerably, and had

suffered proportionately; he was the Ulysses of the new dispensation; he knew mankind intimately—was familiar with all classes; he addressed alike unlettered multitudes and kings and governors, priests and philosophers, the learned, the powerful, the humble, with that perfect self-possession, freedom, and effect which is the singular privilege of genius inspired by faith, and tempered by the gracious air of a man habituated to good society."

"What, now," says our Transatlantic professor of political theology, whose prolegomena we have just listened to, "was the policy of Paul on the point in question, at a future period of his career? That he was well acquainted with the system of absolute servitude, as it existed at the time in Greece and throughout the Roman empire, is obvious. But did he or said he aught to discredit it as an institution? Did he denounce it as unholy, unnatural, or unchristian? By no means. If a slave were a Christian, he

S

was more to Paul than a king; the king, if he
remained a wilfully ignorant pagan, less than
the meanest of his own converted followers.
Paul's policy, then, was simply obedience to all
legal and political authority, whether national
or domestic. Weigh his conduct in regard
to Onesimus and Philemon. Onesimus is the
slave of Philemon, and becomes, like many
others, a runaway—a fugitive slave. While in
this condition he hears the words of spiritual
freedom from the lips of the great Apostle,
to whom the distinctions of social position,
whether as Jew or Gentile, as slave or free, is
a matter of perfect indifference in relation to
the weightier interests of the immortal soul.
He instructs his convert in the way of life, and
treats him altogether in the tenderest and most
fatherly manner. But he bids him return to
Philemon; remembering the social and legal
duties incumbent on each, he returns the now
Christianized slave to his master, with affection-

ate prayers for both. The argument against this peculiar institution as anti-Christian evidently falls to the ground."

Much of this defence is undoubtedly founded on a true basis; but a satisfactory answer to it is found in the fact that slavery in ancient times and in the East, as a social, patriarchal, or domestic institution, is totally different in its main features from the modern institution as exemplified in the West; where it is simply a cruel commercial organization of human machinery for purposes of traffic. The moral feeling of this country against it, there can be no doubt, is therefore thoroughly justifiable; though it sometimes happens that the opinions of strangers, who are witnesses of the comfortable manner in which the domestic slaves are not unfrequently lodged and treated, resembling in this aspect the Eastern or patriarchal system, differ from each other, and from the popular estimate both as to its nature and the extent of the evil.

Were it even granted, for the sake of argument, that the institution itself were not so utterly condemnable on all the grounds assumed by its general opponents in this country and America, yet what may be justly complained of is the total disregard in many instances—often entirely at the option of the proprietor—often at the ordinary junctures of commercial pressure—of those elementary rights which are the distinctive marks of humanity as separable from the inferior orders of nature; the rights of marriage and parentage; the violation of which to those who have any sensibility must be painful in the extreme—to those who have none, brutalizing in the same degree. If a certain respect were shown to these natural rights, and one or two others deducible from them, there would be a ready disposition in the minds of Englishmen to recognise to a given extent the exigencies of a state of society for which the present generation is not exclusively answerable, provided that the labouring and suffering race were not without some attempted alleviation of their lot. But at present it cannot be disguised that an impression prevails on this side the water that both sections of the great republic are equally guilty of much needless and unjustifiable inhumanity towards the black and coloured races; that with a vast superiority of legal and constitutional privileges peculiar to themselves,—with intelligence and education, more widely spread than among any population on the face of the earth, —with a deep and innate devotion to civil and religious liberty,—the community as a whole contrast unfavourably in their treatment of the African and his descendants with the less free, less liberal, less enlightened, and less moral nations of Mexico and Brazil.

If the question of slavery, therefore, be the root of the war—as there can be no doubt it is— it becomes a reasonable inference to draw, that the purification and general amendment of the institution on the one side, and on the other the more liberal and humane treatment of the inter-jacent classes, would constitute the best example they could set each other of a desire to return to a pacific order of affairs. A peace effected on such a basis would indeed be an honour to the whole community, a satisfaction to the kindly feelings of our nature, and a clear gain to universal humanity. England would glory in such a result; and one frequent cause of misunderstanding and bitterness between the various circlets by which the moral and religious world is intersected would be happily removed.

The first duty of the framers of all governments, whose horoscope was so cast as to promise to the native an ordinary degree of longevity, has been to save the people from themselves. This can only be effected by the maintenance of the natural elementary division of society into classes, not necessarily the crude and glaring systems of India or Egypt, but one in which an efficient and self-regulating equilibrium speedily manifests itself, and the primary distinctions of which, as civilization, intelligence, and the moral harmonies of the world expand themselves, become more and more softened into secondary and indeed innumerable varieties. But the distinctions still subsist; and it is no longer a truth clamouring to be recognised, but one acknowledged and appreciated, that it is classes, not masses, that form the true basis of all representative and constitutional government. What the English people would wish to see their Transatlantic brethren enjoy would be a constitution in which there should not be illustrated every imaginable relaxation of political law; a suffrage, for instance, compressed within such limits as should render the holders of it distinguishable; a mode of voting, by which the elector's exercise of his right or trust should be as clearly ascertainable by the public as the

opinions of the candidates; a house of representatives which should exemplify and inter-
pret the opinions and views of the thoughtful,
educated, and intelligent classes of society—
those which ought to be the most influential in
the State, but whose natural authority is unhappily neutralised by the indiscriminate operation, politically, of the immense inorganic mass
of the community, full of impulse, void of conscience; and a senatorial institution which,
being based upon some more dignified foundation than a six years' tenure of office, might be
endowed with the courage and independence
requisite to fulfil the duties of its theoretical
position in rectifying the errors of passion, or
ignorance, or selfishness, to which the multitude
—the majority, it is sad to think—have been
in all ages of the world, and always comparatively must be, liable; but who in this case, by
an anomaly of state polity which it is impos-

sible to justify, are themselves the original
source and ultimate judge of an authority it is
at their option periodically to depose.

Doubtless a more general and more genial
regard exists between England and America
than between any other independent nations in
the world; and it is the sincerest wish of every
true Englishman that the issues of the present
contest may be overruled to the ultimate benefit
of the States themselves, and to the universal
appreciation by both countries of the blessings
and advantages of peace. It is not Oregon,
San Juan, or Ruatan, or any such name, that
stirs up deeply in its fountains the blood of
England or America. If there is ever ill-feeling
simmering in the heart of either, it arises perhaps from the conviction on the part of one, of
the other's persistency in a guilty error, and
expresses itself in the other, in a refusal to
acknowledge as just the somewhat haughty
imputation of the righteousness of an inevitable

sacrifice. But these feelings and the occasion of them will probably pass away without more serious manifestations than such as both have become accustomed to, and which are invariably closed, such is the goodnature of our parental government, by the young republic's obtaining every substantial concession she required. Her "manifest destiny" England acknowledges at heart. But the ways of statesmen are not always the ways of Providence; these are, possibly, wiser than the speculations of the most accomplished minister—more certain of completion than even the least ambitious projects of nations, however intelligent or determined. The ordeal through which she is now passing may not improbably prove to her the process of purification; her exaltation may be in the house of suffering; the scars of sword and fire that now sear her breast may peradventure suggest prudential warnings against future dangers, and serve perhaps as an almost sacred

incentive to the entertainment of holier purposes, and the fulfilment of more venerable
obligations.

Having thus glanced at a fair proportion of
the higher and more prominent objects of public policy, as visible in the intercourse between
our own and other States, it will not be necessary, nor would it be agrèeable, to enter
upon the vast sub-Alpine region of domestic
and colonial legislation. There is only one
movement of any very noticeable features
which has taken place within our borders recently, on which a few observations may not be
inappropriate, because expressive of a change
in the direction of national tendencies, not
only outwardly but inwardly. Nations, as is
evident to even a cursory reader of history, do
not persevere perpetually in the same groove
of policy. Even Destiny seems to step out of her
way. Accordingly as their change is directed
with wisdom and foresight is their prosperity or

decline insured. The world is always old and
always young. As in youth it is the physical
constitution which has first to be developed
and confirmed, all secondary advantages will
follow, God willing, but without health or
strength being but of dubious benefit to their
possessor; so with nations exposed to the
jealousy or cupidity of surrounding Powers, just
sufficiently advanced to perceive the advantage
of those qualities which they do not themselves
possess, the consciousness of being inspired by
the purest sentiments, the nicest honour, the
justest and most generous motives, may eventually prove of no avail, unless capable of being
vindicated promptly and efficiently from any
possible insult by a correlative degree of simple
physical force—in other words, of naval and
military armaments.

Now, the naval force of Great Britain has
generally been, and possibly ought always to
be, such as is capable of bidding defiance to the

world. Her policy has sometimes been, and it may be again, to bid it, and to bide the brunt. But her military forces, exclusive of those required for the distant possessions of the State, are, naturally and properly, used purely for defence.

England has no aggressive schemes in reserve for Europe; she has her own secret sins to answer for, but not that; and can probably never be looked for on the Continent except in the capacity of an ally. But there appears to be an instinctive feeling or premonition throughout Europe, that times of general trouble are in preparation. What grounds exist for such a sentiment do not distinctly show themselves; nor can the quarter be predicted with precision where the decisive outbreak is to occur. This vague sense of uneasiness manifested itself, perhaps, with more acute symptoms in this country than elsewhere; but fortunately, while studying experimentally, as it were, the pathology of panics, England discovered at last an effectual and even agreeable panacea in what may be called the Volunteer tonic: a movement which is deserving of all respect, as an expression of the national will, not only to put itself out of danger, but to preclude anything in the guise of future fear. How it has ramified through all classes, conquered all opposition, converted all scoffers, it is unnecessary to relate. The only novelty in store for us, in connexion with the rifle-movement, that could now effect a "sensation," would be to read in the 'Gazette' of a corps of Quaker artillery, commanded by the Honourable Member for Birmingham.

Simultaneous with this movement, and with the manifestly more warlike tone of the press and of public opinion, as the offensive and defensive armaments of the country have kept gradually but grandly expanding their already colossal proportions, may be undoubtedly noted the subsequent—perhaps it might be said consequent—reaction in the minds of the middle classes against further organic reform, which, if attempted on any considerable scale, can only be effected by the subordination of the general interests of the elective classes to those of one only, whose accession to more than the most moderate degree of power has always been fraught, as history now shows, both in France and America, with the gravest perils. The movement, indeed, may be looked upon as a practical protest upon that matter of the great electoral class; for such a body could never consent to be ruled except by its own representatives.

Thus fortified within and without, England confessedly occupies a more fortunate and formidable position than she has probably ever before held. She has set an example; she has given due warning to the world; she is lavish

in her offers of advice; she is mistress of many
accomplishments: like Pallas, she wields at
home the distaff, abroad the spear. She sur-
veys her well-peopled cities, and her richly-
cultivated fields, and is not wholly unconscious
of her charms, nor indisposed to cherish them
at present in their integrity. "But a little
less spite in her speech," says a voice from
across the Channel; "and a little more con-
gruity between her words and deeds," adds a
guttural-toned orator, still further in the distance, would much enhance her merits and
her attractions. It is not enough that a
press should think openly; it should speak
consistently and judiciously. Yet the English
press, after persisting without any authority in
ascribing to the pen or the immediate dictation
of the French Emperor every violent and reckless pamphlet which has appeared in Paris
during the last three years, now accuses him

of furious despotism in requiring the signature of the writer to this mischievous class of publications. It is not the act of an honest, or if honest, not of a prudent spectator, when nations are struggling with the embarrassments of external war or internal rebellion, when a people are endeavouring to obtain the advantages of constitutional government, to ridicule or depreciate their attempts. Was the constitution of England satisfactorily adjusted at once? Was the representation immediately made perfect? Is there any one ready to die for the belief that it is so now? Nor is it thought kind or considerate to assist in hounding on the pack of insurrectionary cries which usually beset a government at such a moment. It would be better for England, if tempted to such an act, to think of her own condition and conduct in 1798; to reflect, indeed, upon all she has done in Ireland since the days of the truly pious and conscientious

T

Puritans, who desolated it from one end to the other, with fire and sword, and rapine; and then let her blame, with that haughty air and bitter tone, so natural in one whose reputation is perfectly pure, so fascinating in any whose career, like hers, is irreproachable, the mild and dignified forbearance displayed at the present moment by a great continental empire towards a froward, fractious, and selfish member of its dominions. It were better that the foreigners whom we so cordially despise— every nation despises foreigners—each one in his separate version of national events, should not have to record, that while England never hesitated to put down with a mercilessly rigid arm the slightest uprising of rebellion in her own domains, she never scrupled to instigate and justify it in those of even friendly governments; whereby her conduct, history, and propensities seem perpetually and diametrically at variance with each other; for it is not such recollections that will make her friends, when, if ever—which Heaven forefend !—the hour of peril may come upon her.

THE END.

.

LONDON : PRINTED BY W. CLOWES AND SONS, STAMFORD STREET,
AND CHARING CROSS.